PFLAG

Parents, Families and Friends of Lesbians and Gays

P.O. Box 27382, Fresno, CA 93729–7382
(559) 434-6540

You are Welcome! 2:00 P.M. 2nd Sunday
Wesley United Methodist Church, 1343 E. Barstow, Fresno

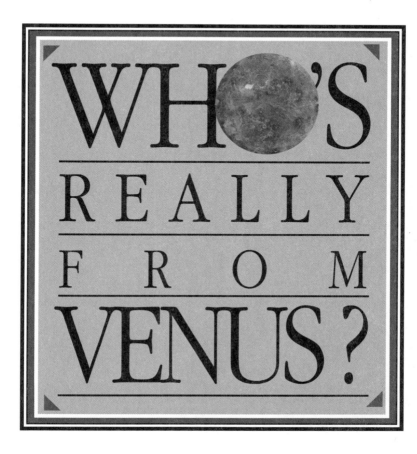

WH☉'S
REALLY
F R O M
VENUS?

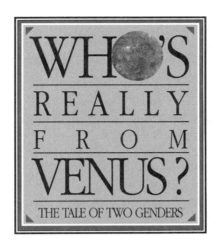

WHO'S REALLY FROM VENUS?
THE TALE OF TWO GENDERS

Peggy J. Rudd, Ed. D.

PM
PUBLISHERS, INC.
KATY, TEXAS

Published 1998 by PM Publishers

Cover designed by Desir`ee Ann Walton, Houston, Texas.

Publisher's Cataloging-in-Publication
(Provided by Quality Books, Inc.)

Rudd, Peggy J.
    Who's really from Venus? : the tale of two genders/Peggy J. Rudd. — 1st ed.
      P. cm
      Includes bibliographical references and index.
      ISBN: 0-962676-24-1

    1. Transvestites. 2. Transsexualism. 3. Gender identity. 4. Sex role. I. Title

HQ77.R83 1998   305.3

                      QBI98-395

In memory of
Ellen Summers
who taught us
the real message of
THE TALE OF
TWO GENDERS.

OTHER
BOOKS
WRITTEN BY
Peggy J. Rudd, Ed. D.

MY HUSBAND WEARS MY CLOTHES:
Crossdressing from the
Perspective of a Wife

CROSSDRESSING WITH DIGNITY:
The Case for
Transcending Gender
Lines

LOVE CALENDAR:
The Secrets of Love

CROSSDRESSERS:
And Those Who Share
Their Lives.

CONTENTS

In Plato's Symposium, man and woman in the sexual embrace, restitute the primary unity of the human person in its fullness, a unity which has been broken. Is the potential for human life as great as the sum total of masculine and feminine traits? The most famous presentation of this concept is found in Genesis when God created man upon Planet Earth.

And God created man in his own image, male and female He created them.

Genesis 1:27

Is balance the desired goal for human life? Could the masculine and feminine characteristics present in each of us link together in harmony to constitute a more perfect existence? Is it possible to experience the best of humanity? Does the process of integration represent the true Tale of Two Genders? This book holds the answers.

ACKNOWLEDGMENTS

*I*n undertaking this book, I was aided immeasurably by friends, colleagues, and loved ones, and I would like to express appreciation for their contributions. I must credit the people who shared their personal accounts for inclusion in *Who's Really From Venus?* I feel a great camaraderie with persons who have walked the same rocky road through life and have found ways to cope. I personally gain insight from the lives of other people. We all seem to face similar challenges.

As the book neared completion, I was assisted by a great team headed by Melanie Rudd and noted editor, Francis Pasek, who skillfully guided my hand. They made certain the information had relevance for professionals and lay persons alike and did the final editing of the book.

I credit Desir`ee Ann Walton for the creative cover design and artistic format. In our conversations, Desir`ee described the pain within the gender community. She expressed a desire to reach out to others around the world with her artistic talent, and willingly gave her time. Barbara Jean greatly enhanced the book with her sketches of feminine beauty. Mel and Tina Schehlein offered encouragement and support. The story of their love has been an inspiration. Their struggle to overcome obstacles was rewarded when they found each other and the symbolic pot of gold at the end of the rainbow.

Last, but certainly not least, I have greatly appreciated the encouragement and assistance from Jane Ellen Fairfax, M.D., who is always a valuable resource. Dr. Fairfax spent endless hours making sure the medical facts were correct, the infinitives were not split, the "I's" were dotted and the "T's" were crossed. It is unusual to have a friend who is a medical resource and a skilled editor. Such a rare gift! Jane has shown, by example, how life can be wonderful, even while transcending Venus and Mars.

We cannot all play
the same instrument,
but we can all play
in the same key.

PREFACE

"Once upon a time Martians and Venusians met, fell in love, and enjoyed happy relationships together because they respected and accepted their differences. They came to Earth and amnesia set in: They forgot they were from different planets."

John Gray

John Gray, in his book, *Men Are from Mars, Women Are from Venus*, used this metaphor to illustrate the commonly occurring differences between men and women. Gray's best selling work is the pre-requisite for *Who's Really From Venus?* which will present another dimension to the metaphor. Some people don't know whether they are Martians or Venusians. This book will unscramble the mystery of why they are a bit of both.

AM I FROM VENUS?

What if the gender lines are blurred? Some women are learning to be assertive and competitive and some men are seeking their softer, more gentle side. This is basic. But the story is sometimes more complicated.

There are thousands of people who have been confused about gender identity for most of their lives. When they begin to find personal answers about gender identity, many wish to make changes in life-style. But, frequently, there is a sudden avalanche of disapproval from observers who want the world to be either black or white. These critics prefer adherence to traditional male or female roles. Gender bending is distasteful to them. They expect children to learn the "correct" gender roles and practice them. Parents provide the props and the name which is appropriate.

Sometimes the expected role is uncomfortable for the child. Very early in life, he may send out some visual clues that the role does not fit. Crossdressers, for example, give accounts of fun exploring Mom's lingerie drawer, or manifest curiosity about lipstick. Many also report the punishment which followed on being caught. *"You were born a boy, and you were taught to act like one."*

The next phase involves the self-inflicted guilt and shame. The child begins to suffer in silence and build a wall high enough to hide his gender preference. Suppressing his cross-gender identity, the little boy begins to act like a typical male. Action complete! A wee Martian, with one foot in Venus, has successfully disguised himself as totally Martian!

Some theorists believe the potential problem began before he was born. The parents visualized how this young life would unfold as a Martian. The rest is a case of mistaken identity and confusion.

As most of us move through life we find gender identity very natural, since it has been programmed for us. For most, assuming the correct gender role is much like breathing. But for a Martian, who must hide his identity as Venusian, there is a disequilibrium. Some perceive a mismatch between their birth sex and the gender with which they identify. There is a vague ambiguity which prompts the question, *"Who's Really From Venus?"*

Let's face it. There are some people who seem to have been born in some unchartered territory of gender. It appears they were born on the border somewhere between Mars and Venus, but not distinctly on either planet. One question remains. What is their real birthright? The issue seems to be complicated at best, and heartbreaking at worst.

SEX AND GENDER

As we search our hearts for understanding of the people who do not totally fit the male or female image, we may find an improved perception of gender and human sexuality. Most of us see ourselves through a gender lens which is socially dictated and enforced. But what if the lens is focused on something other than traditional mores?

Surprise! Sex and gender are not the same! Sex refers to a person's chromosome pattern. Almost all males have an XY chromosome pattern, while an XX chromosome pattern is the norm for females. Gender refers to a set of traits assigned by society. These are intended to distinguish a person as either masculine or feminine. The doctor took one glance at the genitals in the delivery room and announced that a boy or girl had been born. The expectations for their lives were dictated at that moment, with little consideration for those who do not match the stereotype.

Why are some people born with the chromosome pattern and genitalia of a boy and some strong feelings and personal expression of a girl? Where does gender identity originate? How does this adversely affect relationships?

Some people say, "*If it looks like a duck, walks like a duck, and quacks like a duck, then it must be a duck.*" What if a child looks like a boy, and has the chromosome pattern of a boy, but feels like a girl? In rare cases the child may physically resemble a girl in some ways. He may have small hands, soft skin and delicate features. What if the biological and emotional forces are not congruent? These individuals, whether male or female, will need to make significant life adjustments. Keep in mind there are many degrees of variance.

THEORIES AND SOLUTIONS

There are a few theories used to explain the discrepancy between the birth sex and the expression of gender. One theory which has gained some credibility within recent years is the "*Chromosome Push Theory.*" According to this theory, the developing embryo is undifferentiated during the first six weeks of development. At that time the male Y chromosome pushes the gonads to develop along the male genital track. But the embryo will develop along the male pathway only if the correct hormonal signal is received. In some cases the signal is weak and a feminine psyche remains a part of the person for the rest of his life. The discovery of the sex-determining gene has opened doors to new knowledge, but there is still much mystery.

The purpose of this book is to offer some new thoughts about gender. The goal is to help people focus upon human traits, those life qualities that bond us all. This book offers guidance for couples who are working toward happy, healthy relationships which are set within the parameters of cross-gender behavior. Our story begins like this:

Once upon a time Martians and Venusians met, fell in love, and experienced happy relationships. Then they came to Earth, where the roles for gender were dictated by the International Gender Council. The Council was made up of many Earthlings who set the standards of behavior for Planet Earth.

Suddenly, some Martians realized they had the same feelings and emotions as their Venusian lovers. There was no harmony in their love, for an ominous unrest swept over them. The Martians made an appeal to the Extraterrestrial Council.

"Please," they proclaimed. "I was born in Extraterrestrial Gender Space, and have spent my life moving back and forth between Mars and Venus. Help me learn to adjust!" Many members of the Council could not hear their plea, for they had been deafened by the roar of social expectations.

Kohlberg and Ulian believe gender identity is formed very early in life. *"Gender constancy - a sense that a person's gender is a permanent aspect of self is acquired between the ages of three and five years."* Doug Mason-Schrock sees the recollection of childhood memories as worthy of consideration, since this is the time in life in which individuals struggle to mold their personalities. *"Examination of earliest memories that either their sex or gender is 'wrong' or does not fit is valid and significant. These are materials from which individuals mold current identities, and bring the real 'true selves' into being."*

West and Fenstermaker see gender as, *"... achieved in social interaction with others. To achieve accountability as a social actor, one must enact gender in ways that are socially recognizable."* This book will offer new hope for all persons: those who fit the "normal" physical and emotional image and those who seem to be out of step with society. New guidelines will be presented. Coping strategies will be included. People who exist in the Extraterrestrial Gender Space will learn to accept their differences.

This book will offer new hope for all Venusians: Those who fit the physical and emotional image and those who fit only the emotional image. New guidelines will be presented. People who exist in the Extraterrestrial Gender Space will learn to respect and accept themselves. Persons in committed relationships with them will learn to plot a new and exciting course.

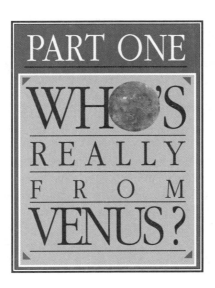

PART ONE

WHO'S
REALLY
F R O M
VENUS?

Mars is the Roman God of war, the husband or lover of Venus, the planet named for him, and the exemplary model of masculinity. Venus is the Roman goddess of love and beauty, the planet named for her, and the model of femininity. But there are millions of people on Planet Earth who chose to embrace the better qualities of both Venus and Mars rather than stay within the stereotypical model or expected norms for their birth sex. Their stories are presented within the pages of this book. The names have been changed to protect identities. The characters of this real-life drama share the same hopes and dreams as other people on Planet Earth. All are looking for love, and some never find it. All are transcending gender lines in their endless journey between Mars and Venus.

This book is about people who challenge the dominant gender system described in the Mars-Venus analogy. Kohlberg sees gender identity as... *"achieved at the interaction level, reified at the cultural level, and institutionally enforced via the family, law, religion, politics, economy, medicine and media. But gender, as an internalized aspect of self is virtually immutable. Those who, for reasons not yet understood, internalize a gender identity that is not congruent with genital configurations, are often sanctioned because they fail to enact gender in socially prescribed ways, thereby challenging the cultural and structural social order."* Huber and Spitz believe the feminist movement and a greater life expectancy have brought us to the threshold of questioning the immutable relationship between birth sex and gender.

The account which follows tells the story of Jennifer, one of millions of individuals in the world who has found a dissonance between birth sex and the expression of gender.

CHAPTER ONE
TRANSCENDING VENUS AND MARS

I met Jennifer in October of 1997. Her beautiful pictures caught my husband's eye as he scanned the internet. We read her story with interest since it seemed remarkably similar to thousands of other stories we have read about crossdressers. All the elements of drama were there: the secrets of childhood, a degree of sibling rivalry, the challenges of college followed by building a life in the real world. While Jennifer's family didn't have much money, her parents did instill in her many values that are absolutely essential to success in life: the value of education, the value of family, and the value of hard work. A favorite family quote was, *"We's poor, but we's good people."* The sociological factors become less important when we look at the big picture of Jennifer's life, for she is the classic example of one who has transcended Venus and Mars.

Bullough described the phenomenon. *"In any society, the perception of femininity and masculinity is not necessarily dependent on female or male genitalia. Crossdressing, gender impersonation, and long-term masquerades of the opposite sex are commonplace throughout history. In the past, however, cross-dressing was practiced more by women. Today men are also attempting to change their public gender. There are many implications for the changing roles in society."*

HOW I CAME TO WHERE I AM: THE STORY OF JENNIFER FITZGERALD

I was born in the Midwest, one of the younger boys in an Irish-Catholic family of ten children. From a very early age it was obvious that I was the sensitive boy in the family. I was bookish, shy and a little chubby. My brothers were more outgoing and athletic when we were kids, but all of us were competing desperately for my dad's limited attention.

When I look back on my parents' life together, I can't imagine what it was like to have that many children around the house! By the time they were my present age, 33, they already had 7 with 3 more to come. As each of us grew into our teens, my brothers went through the typical teenage rebellious phase, but I never did - at least not outwardly. In my early teens I had grown to my current height and had become a natural athlete.

I enjoyed my newfound abilities. I felt the natural exhilaration that comes from athletic success and continued the drive to gain approval from my dad. I excelled in school as well, earning straight A's without really trying. In short, I was the model child, but I was doing well for only one reason: to get attention and approval. Like many children, my entire sense of self-worth was wrapped up in what others, especially my dad, thought of me.

I was harboring a dark secret, too. From the age of nine or ten, about the time I entered puberty, I had a strong desire to wear my sister's clothing. Sometimes I thought I really wanted to be a girl. Many nights, as I knelt next to my bed, I'd pray for God to change me into a girl before I woke up in the morning. My entire world was black and white at the time. If I wasn't a macho male, then it must mean I wanted to be a girl. I was thoroughly confused and ashamed. I believed my feminine desires were somehow wrong, but I couldn't help myself.

Looking back through the years, with the aid of therapy, it seems that I was trying to appeal to my father, who favored my sisters. But, at the same time, I wanted to rebel against him. I knew he wouldn't really approve of my feminine tendencies. But this simple answer doesn't begin to address the full complexity of the issue. I really enjoyed feeling feminine.

I remember the very first time I gave into the impulse to wear my sister's clothes. I was nine years old. There was a powerful burning inside me as I pictured my sister's canary yellow bikini hanging from the towel rack in the bathroom. I lay in bed for hours, wrestling with what I wanted to do. Finally, I succumbed. The whole house was quiet, and my face was burning from the anticipation. I took off my t-shirt, pulled the bikini top from the rack, and held it up to my chest. The thrill that rushed through me was something I had never felt before. It was a mixture of sexual excitement, the knowledge that I was doing something forbidden, and a sense of fulfillment and belonging. I knew I couldn't get out of the bathroom without trying on the bikini bottoms. So with a real sense of resignation, I dropped my jockeys and slowly pulled the bottoms up. It was one of the very first times I ever became physically aroused.

My chances to dress were very limited - as you can imagine with nine siblings in the house. But for the next few years I made a habit of going into the bathroom late at night and dressing up. I grew bolder and bolder.

I was caught by my dad at the age of twelve. I was wearing my sister's mini dress in the middle of the day! Somehow, I thought a closed bathroom door was all the protection I needed. Subconsciously I was probably hoping to get caught. My father was steamed but obviously didn't know what to say. I hid in the basement and cried for hours that day, and I nearly ran away from home.

The next morning my mother had a long talk with me about what had happened and about some strange things she had been noticing. Mother had found my sister's clothes stuffed in the cupboard under the bathroom sink and noted some missing makeup. She questioned me gently. *"Why are you doing this? Do you want to be a girl?"* I was humiliated and ashamed, but somehow I managed to deny everything, and she left me alone after a while.

I longed for her understanding. I wanted to hear the words, *"Wearing your sisters' clothes is not a bad thing! You can dress in her clothes if it will make you feel complete."*

This was one of the points in life that might have changed everything. What if my parents had put me in counseling then? Would I have progressed into a full-blown transsexual with the ultimate journey to surgery and life as a woman? Would I have reached an equilibrium needed for happiness as a crossdresser much earlier in my life?

Although I try not to dwell on the past too much, I can't help but wonder. After that incident, I went several years without dressing again, although a few important things did occur. During that time, I remember watching an "*All in the Family*" episode with a male actor dressed as a woman and hearing the word "*transvestite*" for the first time. I ran to the dictionary in the house, and read the definition. "*A transvestite is a person who has the desire to wear the clothing of the opposite sex or cross-dress.*" Since I enjoyed wearing my sister's clothes the definition seemed to fit me. For the first time I realized that I must be a *transvestite!*

A BREAKTHROUGH IN COLLEGE

I finally realized there must be many more people like me! Maybe I didn't want to be a woman! Maybe there was another lifestyle that would make me happy! I found this lifestyle in college where I had the chance to dress again in the freedom of my own dorm room. But I was still ashamed of my desire because I never wanted to dress partially. Wearing lingerie under my male clothes was not enough for me. I wanted to look like a girl when I was dressed. I fantasized about moving to a different town and living as a woman for a while. Something happened in the fall of my sophomore year which became the first step on the path to where I am today. I met Brooke, a girl from a wealthy, educated family. She had lived in Europe and Africa and had extraordinary poise and maturity for a person her age. She and I became friends in a literature class, and after a few months she asked me out on a date! It was like a veil lifting from my life. I slowly started to pull myself back together. While Brooke introduced me to many of the finer things in life, she was careful to emphasize the value of being a good person.

She and I fell in love, and I confessed what I'd been hiding from her. I was still ashamed of my crossdressing and wanted desperately for it to be taken away from me. Brooke was incredibly understanding, and offered to help me with a feminine image. She also broached the idea of getting counseling through the university health services. Since I believed only crazy people went to therapists, this was a shocking idea! Yielding to her request, I agreed to a short evaluation at the student health services. My counselor was Tom, a specialist in human sexuality and gender issues.

The following six months led me to an amazing time in my life.

The counseling, while painful, came at a crucial time. Brooke helped me purchase a few clothes and a wig, and instructed me in make-up techniques. Finally, the mirror reflected a picture of my true identity. I saw a shy, beautiful teenage girl, the image that had eluded me for years.

Brooke and I began dressing on a regular basis. We even ventured out in her car one time, but I lacked the confidence to get out of the car. We took a lot of photos! Brooke was pleased with the pictures. *"You look so sweet. I'd pledge you in my sorority!"*

The fantasies that came from that one statement could fill volumes. As I began to sort out my life, I came to a big realization. Although guilt was a real threat, I didn't want to stop dressing. Expressing the femme side of me felt good! I needed this outlet. There were parts of my emotional makeup that I denied in my everyday male persona, but these emotions seemed natural when I was dressed. For the first time in my life I felt vulnerability, sadness and the desire to be cared for.

These traits are a part of all of us, but did not seem to fit the masculine stereotype. I came to believe the ideal person focuses more on being human than either masculine or feminine.

The focus of my therapy led me to remove the guilt and shame. I gained control of my obsessive/compulsive behavior. I did not want to yield to impulses. There was a desire to integrate crossdressing into my everyday life, and end the denial. I realized that integration would mean a balance of masculine and feminine traits and such an integration seemed to be an ideal goal.

As in any expansion of consciousness, the process of self-discovery required a lot of time and painful soul-searching. The process expanded my definitions of gender. I saw humanity as a composite of masculine and feminine qualities. People are not two-dimensional stereotypes. This realization represented my first step toward happiness.

Through the next few years, Brooke and I continued to date, and we continued to grow as people. Ultimately, we decided to take different directions in our lives. While our parting was painful, we knew it was best for both of us.

I will be forever grateful to her for expanding my world toward style and elegance. Brooke helped me sort out my priorities, and accept myself as I am. For the first time I truly liked myself and the image I saw in the mirror. I liked the feminine image, but I also came to accept my masculinity. I was beginning to integrate my femininity and my masculinity.

BUILDING A LIFE ON MY OWN

At the age of twenty three I moved to Boston. I'd never been out of the Midwest, had never flown on an airplane, never seen the ocean or a mountain, and was in the middle of a serious financial crisis. My arrival was followed by what I call the Massachusetts Miracle of 1987, since I got a good job right away.

Despite the good fortune financially, I was lonely and forlorn for the first few years. These factors inhibited crossdressing. I sought counseling again, since I needed help with the new expanded boundaries in my life. The therapist, Dr. Joseph Glenmullen, a specialist in sex and gender, guided me toward wise choices rather than living a life paralyzed by fear.

I dated a woman who was broad-minded about life. She helped me dress one time, but because of the weight gain I was not pleased with my appearance. The experience left me feeling discouraged, and the end result was a purge of crossdressing. I got rid of most of my clothes and many of the photos that had been taken in college. In time I came to realize my self-esteem was based on the perceptions of other people and on my day-to-day situation in life. Bad experiences sent my self-worth into a nose-dive.

During the next several months, I began a slow ascent from darkness back into the light. Once again I was faced with the process of putting my life back together. I found a new job, kept up the regular counseling sessions, and started to build a life around how I felt about myself rather than what others thought about me. For the first time I realized my attitude was tied to being a crossdresser. Deep down, I believed I was born with a ten-yard handicap in the race of life. Realizing the need to overcome the negative aspects was the beginning of my ascent to happiness.

Over the next few years I drifted in an aimless search of my purpose in life. The first step involved ending the tendency to worry. This was, by no means, an overnight conversion. During this time, I discovered an amazing rule of life. The less you try to impress someone, the more you end up doing so. I searched for people who cared about who I am rather than how I dress.

Many of the factors that had led me to suppress crossdressing were no longer a problem, and I took charge of my life. Eventually I decided to accumulate a wardrobe and begin dressing again. Shortly thereafter, the stage was set for the most important event of my life. I met Erin, my future wife, at a fund raiser for the Children's Museum in Boston. The first meeting was humorous. A friend of mine was trying to get a date with Erin's friend. We talked while observing the scenario. Both of us enjoyed our visit, but neither of us followed up on it.

Finally, in July, we met again at another fund raiser. This time I told her I wasn't going home without getting a date with her. We danced that evening, I walked her to her car, and kissed her. A few days later I spontaneously proposed. For the first month of our relationship I kept asking her to elope with me to Paris, and she kept treating the proposal like a silly, romantic gesture. After we had been dating for a few months, we went away for a weekend together. This is when we both realized the depth of our love. I also realized it was time to tell her about my crossdressing.

I presented the gender issue carefully. *"There's something important about me that you need to know. I think it's only fair to tell you about this."* I gave her several options. She could make crossdressing a large a part of our life together, or she could be totally uninvolved. My desire was for her to accept crossdressing as an important part of who I am and who I want to be. I was pleased by her reaction. She thought it would be fun! In fact, her mother was a fashion model in the late sixties and early seventies. Erin knew exactly what it was like to experiment with different looks. She thought it was fun to play with makeup and hair styles. Crossdressing wasn't a problem for her, but she expressed confusion about gender and human sexuality. I did my best to explain the Virginia Prince quote, *"Sex is between the legs. Gender is between the ears."*

Erin's interest grew, and she wanted to see me dressed. I was hesitant because I hadn't dressed in nearly six years, and that experience was less than satisfactory. Never the less, we picked a time in which we could experience crossdressing together. We chose a new wig from a catalog and experimented with the wig and make-up. I was amazed and felt anxious to dress fully again. I felt happy and fulfilled when Erin shared this part of me.

There were numerous dress-up evenings including Halloween. We chose our costumes, Miss America and the First Runner-up. Erin graciously allowed me to be Miss America. The reactions we got from our friends were spectacular. Some believed I was a very tall woman. Their expressions were priceless. That small taste of successful dressing encouraged me to seek out the Tiffany Club of New England (TCNE). I had been aware of the club for some time but had never joined. TCNE is a non-profit, support and social club in the greater Boston area. I joined the group, and ventured to my very first meeting in November of 1996. The support and encouragement I got by attending their regular meetings led me to take my first steps out in public.

In the summer of 1996 Erin and I had a story-book wedding on Cape Cod. However, the beautiful event was saddened by the death of my dad at the tender age of 65. I miss him terribly, especially because I finally worked out the issues that were keeping me distant from him. I felt that we had become much closer in the last few years. Finally, there was an awareness of his emotions and struggles.

TODAY AND TOMORROW

In late May of 1997 I visited San Francisco, and brought my femme wardrobe with me. I always love visiting the City by the Bay as it's truly one of the prettiest places in the country. This is a great place to enjoy yourself en-femme. The city offers great shopping, museums, and nightlife. It also gives me a chance to visit my sister, Nancy, and her husband. On this visit my sister agreed to come up to the city and have dinner with me. I had been contemplating telling her about my crossdressing, and discussed the possibility with my wife. Both of us had our doubts. When I'm considering telling somebody about this part of my life, I ask myself four questions:

1. *Is this a long-term relationship?*
2. *Will this person be able to handle crossdressing?*
3. *Can I trust the person to be discrete?*

4. *Will the awareness of crossdressing bring us closer?*

The answer to all these questions must be a wholehearted "*yes*" for me to go ahead. This time Erin and I were not confident the crossdressing would enhance my relationship with my sister, and we were not sure she could be discrete. In my large Irish-Catholic family, as soon as one sibling knows something, we all know it. At least that's been my experience in the past. I wanted to tell Nancy, who's my younger sister by two years. I thought it was a good idea for someone in the family to know, and I'm very close to her.

Nancy came to San Francisco, where I was on a business assignment, and met me at the Hotel Monaco. This is what I would call a "funky" hotel with garish decorations and canopy beds in every room. I had carefully hidden my femme clothes, since I knew Nancy would want to check out the decor. After a warm greeting and a short inspection of the room, she and I went to dinner at the restaurant attached to the hotel.

I was amazed at the turn our conversation took in the first 45 minutes. We always talk about our family, but somehow she was steering the conversation toward the differences between the brothers and the sisters. She had some very insightful observations. I candidly discussed our tendency to interfere in each other's business. Nancy implied that the brothers are guilty of interfering, but the sisters all share very intimate secrets with each other and trust each other to keep them confidential. Stunned by this revelation, I decided to tell her about my crossdressing.

I spent about 20 minutes explaining my gender preference. She was flabbergasted, amused, sympathetic and incredibly curious. Most of her immediate questions were about why I do it, then we moved on to how I do it, and finally to how it fits in with the rest of my life. We rushed back to my hotel room so I could show her some of my clothes, my wig and my breast forms. I had some pictures on my laptop that totally amazed her. She thought of me as her football/basketball playing brother. It was a real shock for her to see what I looked like as a woman!

Nancy was completely supportive, and also expressed the decision to keep this from the rest of the family. Neither of us believe they would reject me. In fact, we are sure our siblings would say, "*Hey, you're still my brother and I love you.*" But we agreed that most of them would feel too uncomfortable. An awareness would probably not bring us closer together, and I have the desire to protect them. I do not want any of my family to feel that they have lost their *"brother"* or *"son"*. They have not!

Before Nancy left that night, she said something that I thought was wonderful. *"Up until tonight you and I have had the regular brother-sister kind of relationship, which has been fine. Now that you've chosen to share this with me, I feel like we've broken through some kind of barrier and gone beyond that. Now we're good friends."* Then she hugged me, kissed me, and said, *"I love you!"* as she headed home. I felt a tremendous feeling of satisfaction and contentment.

Later Nancy told me about the experience of sharing the secret with her husband. According to the account, they stayed up very late that night talking about Nancy's perceptions. In the ensuing days, both expressed compassion. They believe sharing a personal secret is a compliment or tribute to the person who receives the confidence. They pondered the question, *"How well do we really know people?"* My revelation to them led to a re-evaluation of their relationships with others. Their ideas about *"masculinity"* and *"femininity"* have been broadened.

I talked to both of them several times. They have been incredibly understanding, supportive, and comfortable enough with my gender preference to joke with me about it. The next time I'm in San Francisco my sister wants to meet Jennifer! Perhaps we will go shopping. I would like to purchase a canary yellow bikini. Who knows where this road leads? She has a *"brother"* and a *"sister"* - the same person!

You may ask, *"Where are you now?"* Today I am still somewhere between Venus and Mars, but I'm a happily married crossdresser with a wonderful and supportive spouse who says she loves me more because I exemplify the best of two genders! I have shared my secret with a few very close friends. I don't feel guilt or shame over my cross-gender tendencies, since crossdressing has helped strengthen my relationship with Erin and has brought insurmountable joy into my life. Most importantly, I don't regret any of my life's experiences, because each experience has contributed to the growth process. I enjoy my present position in the journey through life and the challenges I face daily as I continue to transcend Venus and Mars.

LESSONS FROM JENNIFER

While the life of each crossdresser is unique, there are many common threads. Most heterosexual crossdressers I have known have experienced some of Jennifer's life script including:

1. *The discovery of the femme side and a temporary desire to hide the truth.*

2. *Guilt related to hurting other people or not living according to expected norms.*

3. *The feeling of being totally alone.*

4. *The desire to purge the need to crossdress.*

5. *Some emotional scars which must be confronted.*

6. *The desire to hide behind macho.*

7. *The pain of rejection.*

8. *Pleasure in seeing and experiencing the feminine side.*

9. *The integration of feminine traits into the male psyche.*

10. *The desire to share the feminine side with loved ones.*

Finding self-acceptance is tedious for those who transcend gender lines. Janice Raymond described the process. *"....although barriers to self-expression and acceptance are declining, trans-genderists continue to grapple with many of the issues that confronted minorities in the United States in the 1970's."*

For many the private expression of gender is not an adequate expression of self. West and Fenstermaker see gender as being achieved and reinforced through human interaction. *" ..the tedium of gender is derived from, and either legitimized or stigmatized by the very superstructure in which it exists."*

DIVERSITY

"Every day we see evidence of strength in diversity- in the work place, in sports, in communities. Too often, however, we see

differences not as a way to expand our talents, but as something that divides us. Respect and dignity must replace intolerance.

History teaches us many valuable lessons. But we must learn to separate ourselves from the past and the prejudices that define those times. The best way to face tomorrow is with an open mind and heart."

Stephen M. Wolf, **Halting the Hatred**

The prejudices described by Wolf have expanded to the transgender community. The book **Bert and Lori** by Robert J. Rowe, describes the reasons for the negative response. *"The term, 'transvestite', or crossdresser, may bring to most people's minds the image of a limp-wristed 'drag queen,' a 'pervert.' or even the homicidal character, Norman Bates from Hitchcock's macabre film, Psycho. But many male crossdressers are, in fact, married and fathers, who dress up in private with the active cooperation, or at least the tolerance, of their wives."*

Some crossdressers need public validation and find fulfillment in the experience of going out in public. The crossdressers who venture out away from the safe, secure confines of home face the greatest scrutiny and criticism, and face the greatest risks. This is also the group that is helping educate the world about the misconceptions related to the heterosexual crossdresser.

While embracing the exemplary model of masculinity, Jennifer experiences life on Mars, the planet named for the God of War. She also considers herself a naturalized citizen of Venus, where love and beauty rule, and people live *The Tale of Two Genders*.

CHAPTER TWO
THE TALE OF TWO
GENDERS

Sex refers to the two divisions of humanity. Men are of the male sex; women are of the female sex. Sex is biological, since our bodies and sexual organs identify us as either male or female. Gender is our mental or emotional identity.

Formulating a valid gender expression is a process that spans a life-time. The journey involves finding an emotional balance that is a comfortable blend of the masculine and feminine traits. Some people, including crossdressers, choose to live *THE TALE OF TWO GENDERS*. While the balance of human traits can be a personality asset, some questions need to be answered.

Why do crossdressers get so intrigued with feminine finery? Part of the answer rests in the basic difference between men and women. Men prefer action; women prefer feelings and emotion. It follows logically that a crossdresser will use the *action* of putting on the clothing as the path toward *feeling* like a woman.

Why do crossdressers feel so compelled to get in touch with feminine emotion? Recent research points directly to genetic factors as the answer to both questions. During the prenatal state all embryos took a hormonal bath which influenced the developing brain. If the hormone-induced process is incomplete, the default female brain may remain a part of the otherwise masculine psyche. Some female characteristics will have a permanent influence.

A portion of the brain may be female. Certainly this fact would lead to the manifestation of some female-typical behaviors. The actions may take on a number of forms, but crossdressing seems to be the most prevalent and obvious. But as crossdressers journey through life, sociological factors are at work as well, and many struggle to understand why there is such a persistent female presence. Although the femme-side may remain hidden for many years, ultimately *she* wants to emerge in all her finery or manifest herself in some more subtle way. *She* wants to be validated.

There is a wide variance in the manifestation of the feminine persona. Some men are able to express femininity with no props. No clothing is needed for them to find the *woman within*. On the other extreme *transgenderists* prefer to live full-time as women. *Transsexuals* may seek sexual reassignment surgery to become women. These degrees of variance indicate some unfinished business within the hormone-induced brain. These theories have been corroborated by a number of researchers including Dr. Milton Diamond of the University of Hawaii Medical School and Dr. Carl Bushong. These noted researchers have found the basic gender pattern exists more or less permanently within our brains for all people. Dr. Bushong lists five attributes that define sex and gender:

Genetic-Our chromosomal inheritance

Physical Appearance-Our primary and secondary sexual characteristics

Brain Sex-Structure of the brain along gender lines

Sexual Orientation-Love/Sex objects, "Love Maps"

Gender Identity-How we see ourselves as male or female.

The pictures which follow depict male crossdressers, but there are also female to male crossdressers. Without the transformation made possible with wigs, makeup and clothing the physical appearance of all the men pictured is masculine, but the functioning brain is *gender gifted*. These men are capable of feeling the emotions of women, as well as the emotions of men. They feel the entire spectrum of humanity! The men pictured are heterosexual, most have been married, and most have fathered children. The photographs are of *Martians who live part-time on Venus*: the president of corporation, a government official, an architect, the owner of a major department store chain, the husband of a famous movie star, and some of the most genuine people you will ever meet. All have faced disapproval to a greater or lesser degree, but feel compelled to live *THE TALE OF TWO GENDERS*.

A CLOSER LOOK AT JENNIFER

Once Jennifer discovered her feminine persona she
was able to get in touch with emotions which did
not seem to fit the masculine stereotype.

Jennifer found the expansion of consciousness to include
self-discovery, and ultimately, the end of guilt and denial.

Jennifer enjoys Halloween as Miss America.
It just doesn't get better than this!

Jennifer - the bathing suit beauty!

VALIDATING EARLY YEARS

Wendy believes it is never too late to be
the *little girl* you always wanted to be.

LOVE AND MARRIAGE

Vanessa and Linda share their love with other
couples who are in transgendered relationships.

CROSSDRESSING AT HOME

Bob, aka Barbara Jean - is a beautiful young woman.

Since growing a beard, Barbara Jean crossdresses
only in the privacy of her home.

A TOUCH OF CLASS

Lori enjoys the beauty, grace and poise
of the classic woman.

It looks like Jami is ready for dinner at the
Windows of the World.

TRANSCENDING VENUS AND MARS

"Your opinion of me will not influence my opinion of you." This is the motto of Jenifer Rene'.

Jenifer Rene' lives a part of her life as Ted.

THE TALE OF TWO GENDERS

Diane is attractive in both the masculine

and feminine personas.

JUST LIKE A WOMAN

Kim is beautiful in classic black.

Gabbi shares a pensive mood.

FUN ON THE DIGNITY CRUISE

Jill won top honors in the passengers' talent show
when she sang, *"Diamonds Are a Girl's Best Friend."*

Jody and her stick pony, Priscilla, Queen of the Seas, lost
the horse race held pool side, but won the hearts
of 1400 passengers on board the Song of America.

Judy proudly wears her cowgirl hat on board to
show she'll always be a Texan.

Brandi wears a beautiful new dress for the
Captain's cocktail party.

A FATHER-DAUGHTER RELATIONSHIP

Dana, aka as David, poses with one of his daughters during the cruise. Both girls expressed acceptance of their father. *"Costumes are just costumes, and a person's personality can prevail even when society falls short of the ideal. Who says Ginger Rogers wears the dress and Fred Astaire wears the top hat?"*

David packed a few *guy* clothes which stirred his daughters' memories. *"When we were children Dad told stories with wise examples, but they were usually about helicopters and oil rigs."*

Dana and her daughter share yet another five course dinner.

Dana enjoys the night on the ship with *her* daughters
and with Melanie's daughter.

OUT AND ABOUT

The driver shows Gail, Melanie, and Chris the
sights in Bermuda.

Tracie and Sara enjoy their first Dignity Cruise.
(Tracie, on the left of the picture, is the genetic woman.)

On costume night it is sometimes difficult to
identify the *real girls*.

Crossdressers or macho men? Who can tell in a toga?

THE EXTENDED FAMILY

During Gail's 80th birthday celebration her niece
gave a special tribute. *"I love you Uncle David.
You are so much like Mother."* Gail sends the
message, ***"It is never too late to be who you are."***

Friends gathered at the famous Lips Restaurant/Club
in New York City to honor Gail on *her* special night.

TWO LOVELY LADIES WHO TELL THE STORY OF GENDER DIVERSITY

Desir'ee Ann Walton, Through Art

Melanie Ann Rudd, Through Publishing

CHAPTER THREE
A DOZEN BITS OF
WISDOM

"When men and women are able to respect and accept their differences then love has a chance to blossom."

From **MEN ARE FROM MARS, WOMEN ARE FROM VENUS** by John Gray

*J*ohn Gray was motivated to help couples understand the hidden differences between men and women. Such an understanding will guide couples toward a more harmonious love. Millions of people experienced an awakening based upon the truths Dr. Gray presented so skillfully. But as I began to write *WHO'S REALLY FROM VENUS*?, I saw a more complex problem.

A typical couple is composed of a woman who enjoys a reciprocal relationship with a man. But what happens if the man also has a very large feminine component and has been aware of the need to express femininity for as long as he can remember? The couple lives in a culture with clear and precise gender lines. Something is wrong with this picture!

Brandi, a beautiful crossdresser from Houston, understands the challenge of forming lasting relationships within the parameters of a unique gender preference. Although Brandi has been married, the relationships were plagued by problems. Recently, I observed a promise ring on her finger and asked if there was a new love in her life. Brandi smiled and said, "*You are right! This is a promise ring. I promise never to get married again!*" The truths presented here can guide many, like Brandi, toward harmonious love relationships. As couples move through the book together, their love will become *as sponges capable of absorbing a greater love.*

ALL ABOUT MARTIANS

Most men I know enjoy doing *the typical guy things*. The crossdresser also enjoys expressing *Venusian qualities*. He perceives himself to be a good citizen, a good provider and an ordinary, good husband in every way except for his strong desire to cross gender lines. Some women are able to move beyond stereotypes and toward the acceptance of the behavior. These women are truly blessed and find a rare happiness.

Other women face major adjustments. Karen, the fiancee of a crossdresser, saw her partner's expression of femininity as inappropriate. She spent her younger years looking forward to marriage and family based upon typical role patterns. As a child she enjoyed fairy tales with "*happily ever after*" endings. Karen was not prepared for life in the gender community. Nothing her mother taught her, and nothing in her socialization, prepared her for the first glimpse of her future husband in a dress. The image did not match her expectations. Karen's initial discomfort is probably related to the perception of males in society. From her earliest memories, she felt the need to find a man who would be strong and fill the role of protector, while she fulfilled her role of wife, mother, and care-giver.

Before Karen knew about the crossdressing, she felt comfort related to her fiancee's strength, and virility. These attributes made her feel secure. But the security vanished like leaves in Autumn when she discovered that her future husband also had a large Venusian side. In time, Karen may discover that masculinity does not vanish with the expression of femininity, but the threat may hang over the relationship in perceptions or reality.

SOLUTIONS

Solutions will not be simple. Few of life's experiences have prepared crossdressers and their partners for blending love with a lifestyle so unique, hidden and unexplained. Those of us who move successfully through the uncharted space which flows freely from Mars to Venus have developed our own system of navigation. Each movement holds new surprises and new challenges. We have, of necessity, become master communicators, determined negotiators, and determined boundary enforcers. We have cried for the loss of our gender identity. We have laughed, partly because the scenarios are so humorous, but also because Shakespeare taught us humor is great in the midst of tragedy.

Despite the challenges, I believe the people who successfully swim these shark-infested waters, and learn to survive, become the happiest people in the world. Perhaps we get stronger when we grow together. Perhaps the added dimensions we share give us added joy. I know one thing; those of us who have made it work are convinced it was worth the effort!

COLIN'S DOZEN BITS OF WISDOM

To my knowledge, General Colin Powell has nothing to do with the gender community, but I believe his twelve rules for life have many applications. General Powell's wisdom has inspired many during recent years. I can personally credit him with a strong positive influence upon my mind and heart.

During a recent cruise with my husband, I finally found time to read. Fortunately, the Powell book was on the shelf when I made my first trip to the ship's library. Within the covers of **COLIN POWELL** I found an abundance of commonsense lessons which were not much different from those my grandfather taught me. I found inspiration to improve my life. Today I still feel the influence. Ironically, the dozen bits of common sense bear a remarkable parallel to the life-skills I have used as my husband and I shared growth in our relationship.

Here are the twelve bits of wisdom provided by Colin Powell. Look at them with more than a quick surface reading. Look with love as the motivation, and personal and relationship growth will be the by-products. Walter Rinder said it well, *" For me, to love is to commit myself without reservation. I am sincerely interested in your happiness and well-being. Whatever your needs are, I will try to fill them. I will give honestly, for if I give dishonestly I receive distrust. I will give you what I need to receive."*

If these rules seem a bit too rigorous for you, have patience. Let these dicta guide you through your lives together.

RULE NUMBER ONE:

It Ain't as Bad as You Think. It Will Be Better in The Morning.

I can hear the roar of disbelief! When we feel a situation is bad, nobody can convince us otherwise. I have lived within the parameters of a relationship that transcends gender lines, and there have been many days that were less than perfect. But as time passed, the negative was miraculously replaced with contentment.

Will it always be *better in the morning*? Overnight improvement may not be possible, but I believe there is hope when we believe in a brighter tomorrow. Our progress toward acceptance is so gradual we may not realize we are growing. Keep on believing. It can happen!

RULE NUMBER TWO:

Get Mad. Then Get Over It.

Good wife! Good husband! We want to appear to be loving and accepting. Getting mad doesn't seem to fit the good wife/husband syndrome. Our efforts to *be perfect* can prevent the open and honest expression of anger. Is it OK to get mad? You bet! But be sure you get mad in a controlled manner. In fact, unless we face these negative emotions, we may never come to grips with all the issues. I do not believe in building a nest of love and living in perpetual anger. Emotions and feelings must be brought out into the open, but *air* your feelings with control, concern for your partner's point of view, and respect for their needs.

Anger does all kinds of negative things to us physically, emotionally, and even spiritually. It is wise to face anger, handle it, and get on with life. Anger is just one letter away from danger. But to say anger does not exist is also dangerous, because suppressed anger is much more harmful than anger confronted.

I have met many wives and partners of crossdressers. Almost all admit to having felt anger at some point in the relationship. This is natural! Anger surfaces when they realize the relationships are atypical. Wives and partners want to spend more time with their husbands and less time with the femme side. They may also get angry about the money spent on crossdressing, especially if there are other more pressing needs. It is easy to feel angry at the whole situation. Feeling angry is O.K. unless it becomes a permanent anger that surfaces often. Constructive, honest, open communication can help couples deal with the negatives. Then you can get on with life, and enjoy an improved emotional state.

RULE NUMBER THREE:

Avoid Having Your Ego So Close to Your Position That When Your Position Falls, Your Ego Goes With It.

We were all born egocentric. Self is the center of the universe. But the element of our being which enables us to think, feel, and act sometimes gets tangled up with those who are closest to us. In the early days of sharing the feminine side of our husbands, we feel that, in some way, we *caused* the behavior. We also believe our own femininity is in jeopardy.

Because of our egocentric nature, most of us have wished the crossdressing could vanish. Its impact upon our lives seems to be negative! Our image is damaged. At some point in the process of growing together, our ego suffers. Most of us know the cross-dressing will not go away. The fact that there is no cure has caused many egos to fall. Solution: *Develop a strong identity characterized by confidence and security.* We didn't cause the crossdressing. We are in no way responsible. We can't make it go away, and we can still remain strong even though the crossdressing is a part of our lives.

The ego problem may exist also for the crossdresser. As in the Pygmalion concept, *her* ego is an *I* problem optometrists can't cure. As the make-up skill improves and the wardrobe increases, the self-centered nature may expand along the wardrobe. The self-made man always tends to admire *her* maker, much as Pygmalion admired the statue which he created. Just remember. If a man gets too big for his britches, the dress won't fit either!

RULE NUMBER FOUR:

It Can Be Done. You Can Live Happily Ever After!

Yes! it can be done. Couples can live happily ever after! Not every day, and certainly not every moment, but we can make it work. I am so pleased during the Spouses' and Partners' Conference for Education (SPICE) as I observe couples walk away arm-in-arm, smiles on their faces and hope in their hearts. There is a wealth of help out there, and when we take advantage of the support in the community and draw strength from one other, we will know our relationships are working. Crossdressing and a harmonious relationship can coexist and thrive together.

RULE NUMBER FIVE:

Be Careful What You Wish For. You May Get It.

Recently on a trip to Corpus Christi, Texas, I read the Ann Landers column while waiting for my flight back to Houston. The column appeared in the **Corpus Christi Caller-Times** and included a letter from a woman who called herself, *"One who has seen it all in California."* This letter caught my eye, for the comments seemed to have great application to the gender community. The letter from California described women who pass up the most loyal, loving, dependable men because of a wish for excitement. California described the scenario. *"I hear about women who put up with men who cheat, abuse, and neglect them. They say they can't find anything better. I would humbly suggest that the problem is not a lack of decent men but an unwillingness to be realistic."*

California believes the women are looking for a man who is charismatic rather than someone who is caring and affectionate. They wish for amusement rather than kindness. *"These women are more likely to wind up with an adventurer who will love them and leave them, rather than a loyal man who will take things slowly and remain devoted. Women who complain that there are no good men should take a look at the ones they passed up."*

According to California, the shy engineer might be a better husband than the handsome sky diver who is long on charm but short on character. Likewise, the qualities women tend to resist in the early stages of love with a crossdresser may be the qualities they find most lovable later in the relationship. Women may be glad they didn't wish away the kinder, more gentle qualities!

RULE NUMBER SIX:

Don't Let Adverse Facts Stand in The Way of Good Decisions.

The myths and adverse facts about the transgendered are out there. Here are a few of them: Crossdressers are weird. Crossdressers are mentally ill. All crossdressers are headed for sexual reassignment surgery. Crossdressers do not contribute to a relationship except disequilibrium and abnormality. All crossdressers are gay. Any woman who would accept a crossdresser is pretty weird herself. Supportive wives and girl-friends are enabling this abnormal, negative behavior. Pietropinto believes there are many male myths and adds this thought, *"To go beyond the male myth, we must reach the real-life male behind the myth, apprehend him in the midst of his ongoing transitions, and explore his thoughts and feelings in all their complexity."* At some point we must put these myths and absurd misconceptions aside and move toward constructive decisions: *Love him. Help him grow. Grow together as a couple. Commit to success.*

RULE NUMBER SEVEN:

You Can't Make Someone Else's Choices. You Shouldn't Let Someone Else Make Yours.

No person can grow by letting someone else make their decisions. This is pretty clear. Wives can't make the difficult decisions for their husbands. Husbands can't make decisions for their wives. But together couples can find the best choices for their relationships. Quickly move away from the power struggle, and toward compromise. Then wise decisions will come easily. Patience may be defined as the ability to make decisions and wait for your partner to make his/hers. Remember that the inability to make a decision is, in itself, a decision. It may not be the decision you are seeking, but it is a decision. This is not too different from the sign on the business man's desk. *"My decision is 'maybe,' and that is final!"* It is choice not chance that sets destiny.

RULE NUMBER EIGHT:

Check Small Things.

Say, *"thank you"* to the person you love for small acts of kindness. If you can't be grateful for what you have received, remember what you have escaped. Work on those little habits which your partner finds irritating, and remember that a *stitch in time saves nine* - even in love. Little things mean a lot to the success of the relationship.

RULE NUMBER NINE:

Share Credit.

In time you will see growth. This will come because of teamwork. Give credit where credit is due. When growth comes, remember that you didn't accomplish the adjustment alone. You probably saw growth in your relationship because of team effort.

RULE NUMBER TEN:

Remain Calm. Be Kind.

Yes! there are times when we really don't feel calm. During those times, take some time out. Think before losing your calm. Get in control of your thoughts and actions. Love is alive only as long as it is nourished with kindness, and understanding.

RULE NUMBER ELEVEN:

Have a Vision.

Dare to dream dreams and have hope. Visualize where you are going and set your sights high. Put on your collective *working clothes* of relationship-building and focus upon reaching the goals you and your partner have set for yourselves and your relationship. Any person can see further than he can reach, but this doesn't mean he should stop reaching.

RULE NUMBER TWELVE:

Have Perpetual Optimism.

Optimism is a force multiplier,
Pessimism will diminish the force.

In a recent **SWEETHEART CONNECTION**, a quarterly newsletter written for the partners of crossdressers, Caryl presented an optimistic view and a parallel pessimistic view from the perspective of the wife or partner of a crossdresser. Caryl believes the pessimist focuses upon the disadvantages evident when *Miss Martian* starts giving makeup tips, and *she* would rather dress up than do the dishes. According to Caryl the pessimist will say, "*I feel frustrated because when my husband, a Martian, invades my Venusian territory, I think I need to put on something 'frilly', but 'she' still looks better than me!*" The optimist believes there are advantages to sharing life with a crossdresser. "*I can experiment with lipstick without having to buy it. The question, 'May I borrow?' has a nice ring to it!*" The optimist feels pleasure in sharing Venus with the person she loves, and welcomes her Martian to enjoy the pleasures of her planet.

Julie Freeman, of California, quotes an old and appropriate cliche and challenges couples, " *...to make lemonade out of lemons. Both of you can learn from each other. Whatever works in the relationship, let it work!*" Julie believes optimists point their faces to the sunshine and seldom see the shadows. In the gender community the optimist is the person who feels we live in the best of two worlds. The pessimist continues to fear this might be true. The pessimist will burn all bridges and then wonder why he can't cross the water. Wisdom comes with experience. As couples move through life, they learn valuable lessons. All of us make mistakes, but as we learn from them our judgment will improve.

There is much speculation about why some Martians prefer to spend time on Venus. When reduced to the simplest form, it all boils down to nature or biological factors versus nurture or the environmental factors. Virginia Prince believes the point generally overlooked by most everyone, including many psychologists and psychiatrists is that we live in a culture that is as "*...highly structured between men and women socially as it is between male and female biologically. However we have little to say about our biology and any variations from normal body structure or function. These are not subject to our conscious control. Society, culture, and gender are all products of the human mind.*" Regardless of the cause, we know there is an impact upon love relationships. We must all go the extra mile. My challenge: *Go ahead and cross the bridge. You may be pleasantly surprised at the joy on the* other side.

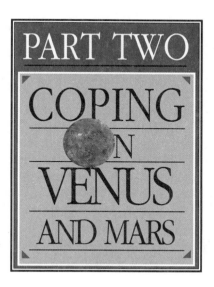

PART TWO

COPING ON VENUS AND MARS

Tewksbury and Gagne' define the trans-genderists as, "...*those persons who enact alternative gender presentations or have internalized alternative gender identities.*" Most crossdressers feel human interaction validates their true identity. But in the process of coming out to other people, some of them do not meet with warm approval, and the rejection they face from people is very painful!

The need for love is as basic as the need for food, water, sleep, and air. Finding love and coping within a committed relationship is not only possible, it is probable when the couple learns to work together. Kierkegard and Goethe describe a sense of continuous struggle, in life, in thought, and in human relationships. The struggle is made bearable when people learn coping skills. The key elements of coping include:

Ending the power struggle,

Intimacy,

Self-acceptance,

Commitment,

Loving unselfishly, and

Holding on to optimism.

CHAPTER FOUR
LET VENUS END THE POWER STRUGGLE

"I hope you have lost your good looks. For while they last any fool can adore you, and the adoration of fools is bad for the soul."

George Bernard Shaw to Alice Lockett

*I*n this quote Shaw is sharing a secret. The beauty of a woman can melt away a man's power. Shaw wishes age would take its toll upon Alice's beauty, make her less appealing, and thus help him regain control. The Shaw quote is a dramatic reminder of the difference between typical men and those who want to emulate feminine qualities. Men who prefer what former President George Bush called, *"the softer more gentle side,"* have a different motivation for admiring a woman-they want to be like her. *Femmiphile*, a word coined by Virginia Prince, literally means, *lover of the feminine.* The beauty of a woman will inspire a femmiphile to dig deeper into his psyche in order to perfect the feminine side of his personality. By so doing, he is letting Venus end the power struggle, for Venus is the planet of peace.

THE BEST HUMAN QUALITIES

Unlike Bush, Jon Winokur, the author of **CURMUDGEON'S GARDEN OF LOVE**, agrees with Shaw, and extends the fear of losing power into the context of marriage. According to Winokur, a man loses some of his power when committed to a woman. "*The fundamental trouble with marriage,*" writes Winokur, "*is that it shakes a man's confidence in himself, and so greatly diminishes his general competence and effectiveness. His habit of mind becomes*

*that of a commander who has lost a decisive and calamitous battle.
He never quite trusts himself thereafter."*

The fear experienced by the man who has *one foot in Venus*
may be somewhat different from fear described by Shaw and
Winokur. He prefers to share strength with the woman he loves
while drawing strength from her. But when other people expect
him to exemplify the typical macho characteristics there is an
uneasy feeling; a disequilibrium. Some days he feels more gentle
than robust and more caring than dominant. Confidence fails when
he attempts to act upon the expectations of other people rather than
follow his heart and his emotions. An inner conflict is not uncommon for the man who is searching for self-actualization through an
integration of *the best human qualities.* Although he has the desire
to fulfill expected roles, he also desires balance and harmony. The
Venusian qualities, including compassion, nurturing and caring feel
natural, but social stereotypes dictate that he should be more
masculine. He has been programmed to believe in masculine
superiority, and he does not want to be labeled unworthy of his
Martian heritage. Conformity seems to be the easiest path.

Sharing life with a man with *one foot in Venus* may be a very
difficult adjustment for some women, since they have been taught
that strong, dominant males are best prepared to provide for the
family. Ironically, the more compassionate man may enjoy a very
successful career if he is able to integrate decisiveness with
compassion. The balance of masculine and feminine qualities make
him a more effective leader. This is the reason I advocate integration of all aspects of the personality rather than the practice of
being either *all woman* or *all man.* It is far better for men and
women to be *all human.*

Some fortunate men are able to enjoy observing the finer
feminine qualities within the personalities of the women they love
and translate the observation into an improved personality for
themselves. By the same token, women will be stronger and more
effective when the better masculine traits become a part of who
they are.

Anne Moire, in her controversial best seller, **BRAIN SEX**,
describes the traits traditional men find appealing, and the list
contains no Venusian qualities. "*Overwhelmingly the characteristics chosen by men include being shrewd, assertive, dominating,
competitive, critical, and self-controlled.*" These are the traits

which exemplify Mars. "*Most men*," according to Moire, "*value competence, scientific toys and principles, prestige, power, dominance, and freedom.*" But is typical behavior ideal? When individuals, male or female, have integrated both masculine and feminine traits, they may place less value on power while enjoying the feminine amenities such as aesthetic beauty. Venus is a "*world of feeling.*" Problems arise when the crossdresser holds tenaciously to one side of the personality at the expense of the other side. Balance is the key.

Woody Allen probably questions the idea of projecting feminine traits, since he has taken a strong stand for masculine superiority. He openly expressed the inferiority of a woman in his life. "*For the first year of marriage,*" says Allen, "*I tended to place my wife underneath the pedestal.*"

My experience with love is in stark contrast to Allen's view. I have never been placed "*under a pedestal.*" When I was a young girl, my father placed me "*on a pedestal.*" I felt appreciated, admired, and loved, and free to express the better traits from Mars including leadership skills and competence, as well as the better feminine traits of empathy and compassion. Even today, the men I admire most are very different from Woody Allen. I admire men who are balanced and in harmony with themselves. Such men find it easy to appreciate, praise, and exalt the women of their lives to the point of emulating their better traits.

THE STATE OF WOMANHOOD

Where do these views about superiority originate? Some of the theories originated with Freud who saw the power struggle between men and women as a simple difference between the sexes. Note the words of Freud:

"*No prohibition shatters her love for her father, but she learns that she possesses nothing with which to implement it. A sense of her inferiority sets her on the path to femininity. The girl's positive love for her father is entered into by default; it is not as strong as the boy's Oedipus complex nor is there any reason fully to give it up. On the contrary she finds her cultural place in a patriarchal society when she finally manages to achieve love for her father.*"

The views reflected here explain why crossdressers find it difficult to gain acceptance. Based upon the words of Freud, there is little wonder society does not understand people who transcend gender lines. I can hear the collective voice of society. "*If he was born a superior male, why would he choose to emulate an inferior female?*"

Gail Sheely, in her book **PASSAGES**, takes this idea one step further as she asks a very provocative question, "*Why can't a woman be more like a man, and a man less like a racehorse?*" Sheely answers her own question in a very simple manner, "*Men must. Women don't have to.*"

Sheely continues her explanation in this way:

> "*A woman doesn't have to find an independent form in her twenties. There is always a back door out. She can always attach to a stronger one. She can become the maker of babies and the baker of brownies, the carrier of her husband's dream. If she resists this pattern, she runs into the contradiction between permissions for development given to men and women. The achieving woman has always been exposed to intimidation by the same threats that hang over the underachieving young man.*"

In recent years the struggle for power has involved women who refuse to be *somewhere beneath the pedestal* where Allen placed his wife during the first year of marriage, or the carrier of her husband's dream as Sheely explained it. A woman has other options. She can choose to be superior; she can move forward with her own dreams. A woman can also choose to be the best person possible within the range of her abilities. Charlotte Whitton, former mayor of Ottawa, expressed how difficult the climb to the top may be for women. "*Whatever women do they must do twice as well as men even to be thought of as half as good.*" The most important point is for her to be satisfied with her own accomplishments. Self-satisfaction is more important than approval from others. If the pendulum swings the other direction to make women feel superior, or seek to be superior, there is still a problem.

LOVE AS A PARTNERSHIP

I perceive love to be more a partnership than a competition or a struggle for control. In a world of power, diplomacy can not afford sentimentality. Power refers to any physical, mental, or moral capacity, whether used or not. In the ideal love relationship there is a balance of power. Neither person should use force to impose his will upon the other.

Jimmy Cannon said it this way, "*I judge how much a man cares for a woman by the amount of space he allows her under a jointly shared umbrella.*" Cannon is describing sharing and cooperation.

Love is not about power. It is about sharing everything from the umbrella to the total fullness of life. Relationships should never become a stage on which dominance and submission are acted out. Actually, according to Phillis McGinley, "*Women are not men's equals in anything except responsibility. We are not their inferiors either, or even their superiors.*"

According to my own view, successful relationships are characterized by a shared power base. Henry Kissenger was a little closer to truth when he said, "*Nobody will ever win the battle of the sexes. There's too much fraternizing with the enemy.*"

Remove the word, *enemy* from Kissenger's quote and we may have it right. Persons in love are on the same team, fighting the same battles, and facing life together. In an ideal world, Martians and Venusians coexist in harmony, sharing the better parts of each other. They are not enemies!

SOME THOUGHTS ABOUT TEAMWORK, PARASITES, AND TYRANTS

What is the impact of power within a love relationship? I have observed relationships that fail even when power is balanced while other relationships succeed even in the face of a power imbalance. Let me clarify. While it is unusual for relationships with a lopsided power base to work, success is possible if both agree about who has the power. Some people are more comfortable letting another person make the decisions, stay in control, and lead. This is not too different from organizations in which some people choose to follow the lead of others, whom they perceive to be more efficient or knowledgeable.

In most cases a shared power base works best; but if such relationships fail, you can be sure other negative factors are at work. Oliver Goldsmith described love as, "*an intercourse between tyrants and slaves,*" and termed friendship, "*the exchange between equals.*"

Did Goldsmith realize that ideal lovers must also be friends? Did he believe the relationship between tyrants and slaves is characterized by love? I believe love requires mutual respect very different from the relationship between tyrants and slaves.

Ian Shoales perceives an imbalance within love. "*The word 'relationship' best refers to the connection between parasite and host, or shark and remora. It's a biological term. I'd rather be a jerk than a scientist when it comes to love.*"

My college biology classes defined a parasite as a plant or animal that draws life from another plant or animal. The parasite cannot exist separate from the host. We frequently describe people as parasites if they live off the kindness of others without making any useful or fitting return. We sometimes call them the "*hangers on,*" like the remora, which attaches itself to a shark in order to gain a free ride.

I tend to disagree with both Goldsmith and Shoales, because I believe love will be more permanent when each person contributes. Relationships work best when people involved base their time together upon equality. Even when couples are not equal in physical strength, intelligence, or prestige, they can still be equal partners in marriage. When the power is shared, couples will usually find more success together.

When competition enters the picture, each person tries to better his own position at the expense of the other. Individual standing takes precedent. Energy is used to gain superiority rather than care for each other. The emphasis is upon being in charge rather than cooperation. Such attitudes are an antithesis to love.

Let me use physiology to illustrate the value of cooperation. My right leg is stronger than my left leg. I can kick a ball further with my right leg, but this does not make me want to stop using the left leg. I would have a difficult time walking with only one leg. Men are born with bodies that are usually stronger than the more fragile bodies of women. This does not cause the woman to be inactive within the relationship or the man to be more active. The couple continues to work together. An interesting fact remains. Men are stronger, but women usually live longer than men. So we are back to the original question, *"Who's really from Venus?"*

Women and men can do more together than either of them can do alone. It is teamwork which is far superior to dominance. In the spirit of love a man and a woman may share their lives together in an environment of harmony. There is little they cannot accomplish as a team. Two heads and hearts together are better than one. Inequality does not invalidate team effort.

For example, vision exams have proven my right eye to be stronger. In fact, the left eye is legally blind without correction. The optometrist corrected the weaker eye for reading and the stronger eye for distance by using a system known as mono vision. Something very interesting happens when I wear my contact lenses. My two eyes perform automatically. I never know which eye is working for me at any given moment. They switch back and forth, each performing their assigned function, without any conscious effort on my part. Sometimes, however, I misplace one of the contacts. When this happens, I am very aware of which contact is missing. If it is the left one, I can not read. If it is the right one, I can not drive my car.

Just as a lazy eye becomes weak from disuse, a person must be actively involved in the relationship. Love should be like my contact lenses. Lovers should never make an issue of strength or weakness or who does what or who doesn't fulfill a certain responsibility. Each person should continue to do whatever it is they do best to the best of their ability, and work harmoniously as a team. If you don't think cooperation is important watch what happens to a wagon when one wheel comes off! When we share each other's burden we are both able to walk a little taller. To say this another way, freckles would make a great tan if they could just get together.

THE PROBLEM WITH DOMINANCE

When one of the partners is dominant, there can be an unhealthy blend of control on the one hand and dependency on the other. The dependent partner tends to lose the feeling of value and self-worth. In time he or she may become incapable of making decisions. Meanwhile the person with power may be making all the decisions with little concern for the other person's desires or preferences. The submissive partner may attempt to provide input, but they may be interrupted by the dominant partner. *"What are you talking about? That would never work and you know it!"* This perpetuates the feeling of inadequacy.

WHERE DECISIONS ABIDE, SO LIVES THE POWER

One of the best ways to determine who is really in control would be to observe the decision making process. Does one person make the decision and impose them upon the other? Ideally, the decision is jointly made after determining the preference of each individual. If there is disunity while the decision is being made, the stage is set for a battle. It is interesting to observe couples who actually don't know who is in control. Many women will say, *"My husband is clearly the head of the household!"* But when the couple gets to the decision making process we see Margaret Thatcher and Casper Milquetoast. The little woman holds all the cards and exerts all the authority.

Who, for example, was in control of the Edward VIII and Wallis Simpson relationship? He obviously had the power of the world at his fingertips, but she wrote these words to him, *"I am so anxious for you to not abdicate, and I think the fact that you do is going to put me in a very wrong light to the entire world, because they will say I could have prevented it."* If we knew whether or not she could have prevented it, we would know who actually had the power. The woman in control is one who can get her husband to listen to reason or anything else for that matter.

LOCATE THE STRENGTHS

Ideally, couples will look for the strengths of each other and capitalize upon them. For example, one person may have a talent for interior design. It might be best if this person makes more decisions about how the home is decorated. The person who is more organized is better suited to keep the file cabinets in order or plan where and how things are arranged within the storage areas. It is best to recognize strengths, and use them for mutual benefit.

Most relationships work best with each person doing the tasks he or she does best. My husband and I share responsibilities, especially at airports, since we travel a lot. Each of us has areas of responsibility based upon preference and ability. We get through the tedium of travel with few headaches.

LOCATE THE WEAKNESSES

If it is important to recognize strengths, it is equally important to recognize the weaknesses, those aspects that can be a liability when not addressed. Not recognizing problem areas can lead to a communication impasse. It is so beautiful to have a relationship strong enough to deal with problem areas without undue sensitivity and with a desire to improve.

A dangerous situation occurs when one or both of the people play upon the weaknesses of the other. It is a joy to extend a helping hand and see the person you love grow beyond weakness. Grow together and not apart Somewhere in your heart find the courage to adjust to the weaknesses of each other, the vision to welcome another chance, and the confidence to stay out of step when other people seem to be marching to different drummer. Successful relationships are like golf. Forget the score and keep on swinging!

FIVE WAYS TO LET VENUS END THE POWER STRUGGLE

In an ideal world, people integrate the best traits from Venus and Mars. People focus upon the peace exemplified by Venus rather than war which exemplifies Mars. The ideal person strives to be the *best human* possible. The better qualities of Venus, including kindness, compromise, and compassion are blended harmoniously with the better traits from Mars, the planet of accomplishment, orderliness, and nobility. Once this goal is achieved people in committed relationships are ready to let Venus end the power struggle.

Relationship therapists have been telling us for years that couples who move toward an integration of both masculine and feminine characteristics have fewer adjustments when they enter a committed relationship. Unfortunately men who focus upon their masculinity to the point of being overly robust and virile are usually attracted to the femme fatale. The resulting relationships tend to be polarized and predictable power struggles will probably keep these couples in a state of constant *war* once the novelty has worn off. The couples with the least possible conflict will exemplify the better qualities of Venus and Mars. Such couples will have a basic understanding of relationship issues; the motivations and the actions.

Follow these five steps as you seek to improve yourself as a person and as a partner in a love relationship. First, share the power base. Second, be aware of the powers of dominance. Third, recognize the strengths of each other and use the strengths for mutual advantage. Fourth, recognize the weaknesses of each other, but refuse the liability of the weaknesses; use them as an avenue for growth. Fifth, let the better qualities of Venus and Mars flow through you.

Men of genius are admired; men of wealth are envied; but only men of character are trusted. Power is dangerous unless it is coupled with compassion and humility, for a compassionate man wields more power than a man with muscle. This will be a better world when the power of love replaces the love of power. Move from the love of power, toward empathy, and a concern for the well-being of others. Then a higher level of trust will be born. At that time we will be able to answer the question, **"Who's really from Venus?"**

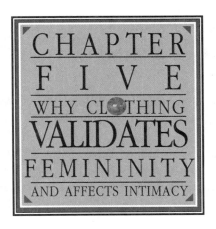

CHAPTER FIVE
WHY CLOTHING
VALIDATES
FEMININITY
AND AFFECTS INTIMACY

*I*met Jan for the first time one stormy day last spring. Beneath her tear-streaked face, there was a softness which was somehow lost in the magnitude of pain she felt at that moment. The storm outside did not begin to compare to the hurricane in her heart. "*I thought my husband and I had no secrets,*" she confided. "*We talked about all aspects of life. At least that's what I thought until last week.*"

Jan's confidence in her husband and in her relationship had been shattered. She found Ken's suitcase of feminine clothing and discovered that he was a crossdresser.

"*I did not have a clue there was another side to Ken. I actually believed we had the perfect marriage, and I thought I knew him very well. But he completely hid the crossdressing from me. Now I am wondering what other secrets he has kept. I feel betrayed, hurt, angry, and totally alone for the first time in twenty years.*"

Jan believed she and Ken had enjoyed true intimacy, the kind of relationship characterized by mutual trust and candor. "*I felt so close to him! But now it seems the foundation of our relationship is damaged. I am afraid we may have a serious problem. Honesty, and sharing are very important to me, and Ken has not lived up to my expectations in these areas.*"

Ken made the decision to keep his crossdressing a secret. This deliberate decision was based upon his awareness of the risk of rejection from family and friends. Having observed other cross-dressers suffering the intense pain of rejection, he feared the loss of the love of his life, and concluded that the pain of rejection was probably the most prevalent heartache within the gender community.

THE RISKS OF INTIMACY

In the process of writing **CROSSDRESSING WITH DIG-NITY** in 1990, I surveyed over 850 crossdressers. The data show fear of rejection to be the number one reason for withholding information about crossdressing. Ken agreed with the data, and expressed his thoughts. *"A person can live with physical pain. People can also handle sorrow, frustration, and failure, but when the person we love turns away from us there is an intense pain no analgesic can remove."*

Ken, and other crossdressers like him, made the difficult decision to live in secrecy. Secrecy seemed to be a better option than the potential loss of his beloved wife.

When we open our hearts to another person, the experience can be painful for another reason. Sharing secrets can cause an introspection that stirs our passions. Through the years we hide some aspects of our life because it feels "safer". Tucked away deep inside, our secrets are hidden rather than open for scrutiny. When we confront these hidden aspects of our psyche, and attempt to grow beyond them, there is surely going to be pain.

Ken was forced to examine his life after Jan found the clothes. It soon became evident that he had not faced the crossdressing issue with full self-awareness and self-confidence. His own lack of understanding had caused guilt and shame, which played a part in his decision to keep the crossdressing issue a secret. He feared a lack of acceptance from Jan because he had not fully accepted himself. In some ways the pain Ken felt was similar to the discomfort he had experienced after a few too many leg lifts or added weights in the exercise room.

When people start to develop new muscles, there is a feeling of strain. Growing emotionally hurts, too. An emotional commitment can lead to growth if we are truly open and honest, both with ourselves and with the persons we love. Ken had been forced into an honesty which was long overdue.

True intimacy developed for Jan and Ken during the months which followed. They helped each other grow stronger. Ken told me the experience reminded him of the ancient proverb which stated, *"Master yourself and you can master anything."*

SHARING OF SELF

Intimate relationships are incomplete until each person is willing to be open and honest. For a crossdresser there is a great fear related to sharing secrets, hopes, ideals, and dreams, but a sharing of self is the measure of intimacy.

Are you able to say anything, or do anything with your partner without fear of rebuke? Can you put yourself into a vulnerable position without fear? You have found true intimacy if you never worry about how immature, ridiculous, or silly you might appear, or whether or not you are living on the right planet. Such a comfort zone provides a sense of safety and security.

Frequently, crossdressers ask a very basic question, "*When should I tell the woman I love that I sometimes visit Planet Venus and feel the emotions of her world through clothing?*" Probably the time is right for married crossdressers when there is open communication within the relationship. If a crossdresser is becoming seriously involved in a relationship and is considering marriage, this may be the time to share his "secret". Having a good sexual relationship will not guarantee that the partner is ready for the introduction of crossdressing.

True love is a unique form of passion. It acquires a stereoscopic perspective, a depth as well as height and breadth. Ideally, it takes up more space in the head than in the bed. There is a profound difference between sex-love and mind-love. All too frequently sex-love is dominant, simply because of the selfish nature of people and the tendency to rush into a relationship before there is a foundation for it. Couples should strive for a balanced love with just the right portions of each.

Inevitably, when crossdressers enter a love relationship they must ask the same questions Ken had asked himself. "*Do I tell her and risk losing her, or do I continue to hide beneath the veneer of macho and hope she never finds out?*"

Some, like Ken, feel the risk is too great, and they continue to hide their secret for years. In time they may find the secret to be a burden. It is so much better to have someone at your side helping you carry the load. Secrets are similar to an aching tooth. It keeps you uneasy until it comes out!

INTIMACY ON VENUS

Another problem emerges when couples begin sharing an intimate relationship. Many men and women do not always agree about ways to express intimate feelings. Frequently the Venusian desires more intimacy than the Martian. Girls are taught at a very young age to share feelings openly. Boys, on the other hand, may be taught to hold feelings inside. Ken fit this profile. Unfortunately, his lack of openness resulted in great pain for Jan as well as for himself. Crossdressers, like Ken, should re-think the traditional Martian stereotypes. Ken expected acceptance from Jan when he began to express the Venusian persona, yet he was holding tenaciously to the typical Martian profile. This included a reluctance to express affection.

If crossdressers claim to be from Venus, they should permit more of the positive feminine qualities to become a part of their personalities. All too often, crossdressers assume the nicest parts of femininity while insisting on all their male prerogatives. This scenario breeds resentment. Given this double standard, can the wife carve out an identity for herself?

Wives grow more accepting when they see positive fruits spring from their husband's feminine development. I believe acceptance comes easier for a woman when the crossdresser's femininity becomes more than pretty clothes. Integration is something one strives to achieve, and there are no shortcuts to integration.

Most Venusians are not much different from Jan. They want their Martians to talk to them more, listen to them and be honest. Venusians enjoy talking! Some Martians tend to hide their feelings and prefer to act out what they think and feel rather than talk about it. As the old song says, *"Your lips may be near, but where is your heart."*

WHY CROSSDRESSERS NEED TO WEAR FEMININE CLOTHING

Martians communicate through doing. *"You like flowers, so I will clean your flower beds for you."* She would rather work on the relationship and hear the words, *"I love you."* This is an excellent answer to the question, *"Why do men need to put on dresses in order to feel feminine?"* Quite possibly the reasons are tied to their preference for action. Martians have *doing brains* as indicated by this schematic:

1. Some Martians may find it easier to *act* feminine than to *feel* or *communicate* in a feminine manner.

2. Therefore, Martians living on Venus look for practical solutions. I want to express femininity, so the *practical* activity is wearing Venusian clothing.

3. Martians depend upon visual clues, so it follows logically that crossdressers love to have their pictures made and frequently glance into the mirror.

4. Some crossdressers enjoy being seen in public while in the femme role because visibility validates their femininity.

5. Wearing silk underwear is a reminder that the femme side is always present. Its message: *"I am proud of my femininity."* Action complete! Clothing has bridged the gap between Venus and Mars!

There is an interesting twist to this scenario. I know a few crossdressers who believe they have reached a new level of *acting* feminine when they have thirty pairs of shoes and a drawer full of jewelry. For some there appears to be an element of Narcissism when endless hours are spent in front of a mirror admiring the finished product. Often wives complain, *"We have no sex life, because he has fallen in love with herself."* Thus, the new level of crossdressing activity is not contributing anything positive to the love relationship.

Glen Midgley seems to be the exception to this behavior. *"When I got in touch with the feminine emotions and started to feel feminine, I also learned to communicate my femininity better. The clothes, per se, are not as important anymore, because I have moved away from the act of crossdressing and toward the feminine practice of acknowledging my feelings and emotions."* Unlike Glen, acceleration seems to be the norm for most crossdressers.

Glen knows his theory will be unpopular for those who can not yet perceive the concept of gender balance. It seems he has moved to a total integration of the masculine and feminine components to his personality. He does not need an *action* to get in touch with his feelings. In addition to preferring action over communication the typical male also needs space. I know some crossdressers who reserve the feminine persona for their own private pleasure and fear sharing this important part of themselves with their wife or partner. Ken admitted his tendency to be secretive and also acknowledged that the motivation was sometimes selfish.

Barbara Jean, who prefers to project masculinity by wearing a beard, enjoys holding crossdressing activities as a very private affair. She spends endless hours in seclusion, sketching pictures of feminine beauty. The sketches represent Barbara Jean's inner love for her femme-side. The art is an expression of who she is. Generosity is the motivator, since the art is frequently given as gifts to friends and loved ones. She seems to be saying, "*I am giving you a part of myself.*"

Many men, including some crossdressers, may find it difficult to express their feelings and emotions verbally. It is easier for them to demonstrate love with actions, such as the art, than to express love with words. But the original commitment between couples goes beyond this concept. Intimate love needs to be communicated both verbally and non-verbally. Holding the love inside the heart is never enough. Go ahead. Show it! Love is like medicine. It doesn't work until it is out of the bottle.

Intimacy requires energy, especially if the couple is learning to accept each other. The crossdresser is constantly learning to accept new dimensions of himself. The woman he loves is altering her previous conceptions about love, sex, gender and a committed relationship. She has to make a lot of adjustments. The more the crossdresser pushes her toward alien surroundings and values, the more difficult the adjustment will become.

Jane Ellen, a crossdresser and the leader of one of the world's largest support organizations for crossdressers, agrees with these ideas and shared her experiences. "*My wife, Frances, has accepted Jane, in part, because Frances was able to maintain her values. She can still be a woman, married to her man, who happens to be a crossdresser. I am also a Christian, a loving husband and a caring and giving father to our two sons. I enjoy expressing my feminine side. That, and 'Gender Land Politics' is all to which Frances has had to adjust."*

THE VALUE OF INTIMACY

As couples face the challenge of adjustment it is important that individuals have a similar need for intimacy. When one person craves more than the other, there is an imbalance that breeds potential problems. Acceptance will be delayed if not aborted completely. As a general rule, Venusians require more expressions of affection than Martians. Perhaps crossdressers could learn more about femininity by observing the women in their lives. When crossdressers model a more open expression of affection, they are closer to being typical Venusians.

Life spent in a rich, fulfilling relationship is the most satisfying human condition. When the individuals seek mutual well-being rather than selfish interests, there is a reciprocal effect. Happiness seems to come back to the giver. To determine whether you have this kind of relationship, look at the motivation for your actions. Do you seek the relationship for your own good, the good of your partner, or the good of the relationship? Do you seek mutuality?

Is it possible to give up your preferences and desires too much of the time? Demanding your own way too frequently is damaging and can lead to the end of a relationship. Sacrificing all your hopes and dreams can also be destructive, because this leads to the *poor me syndrome. Pity parties* are lonely affairs. Selfish motivation and excessive sacrifice will end with a short circuit.

Look for balance in your life and in your demands on others. Love will be tested in the crucible of time and circumstance.

MY MOTTO

The foundation of true intimacy is based upon this motto:

In our love I want to be an instrument of peace.
Where there is a problem I will scatter love.

Where there is offense I will bring pardon.

And I will permit the love of my life to help me grow.

I desire union instead of discord.

Praise more than criticism.

I will willingly do my part to build the self-esteem of my wife or partner.

I will be faithful, helpful, and I will love unconditionally.

My thrust will be truth instead of error.

Hope instead of doubt,

And joy where once there was sadness.

Not only will I crave to be loved,

But I will love unselfishly.

For in giving I will receive.

And in forgetting self I will find another.

For once we have found intimacy,

Together we will find a more beautiful life.

THE DECISION TO LOVE

Most people agree that a mutually loving relationship is the most fulfilling aspect of life. Understanding this will add much insight. Last fall my husband and I sat by a roaring fire and listened to some of our favorite songs. Caught in the rapture of the moment, I said, *"I chose to love you, and what is equally important, I chose to continue to love you when you told me about your gender preference."* At first that sounds a bit cold and calculating, but actually my mental decision was controlled by my heart as well. I know our intimacy guided us toward mutual respect, love for the "total" self and honesty. These attributes became our foundation for coping with the issues we face in our marriage and relationship. We have not permitted crossdressing to negatively affect our relationship.

Intimacy as described here, involves much more than sex. In one context, to be intimate may mean becoming very familiar with someone, or to know him very well. Enduring relationships are based upon this type of closeness. Couples who are successful in their relationships develop a form of self-sharing prior to sexual intimacy, but avoid these pitfalls:

1. *A relationship based upon feelings.* Feeling, when standing alone, will be a weak foundation for lasting love. Feelings come and go. Some days we don't feel very lovable nor do we feel like loving another.

2. *Relationships based solely on passion.* Relationships based upon passion are usually short-lived. Passion may even be a destructive force when there is no foundation for the sexual attraction. Passion will not be sufficient to overcome the obstacles most couples face.

3. *Sexual intimacy without emotional intimacy.* Sexual intimacy without love represents a very weak fiber from which to build a relationship.

When intimacy of the heart precedes the intimacy of the body, our human sexuality will be placed in proper balance. If, however, there is no real foundation for sexuality, the fire of the moment will turn into vapor and dissipate as quickly as it came. Similarity or temperament will remain more constant. A determined love, characterized by self-awareness and mutual understanding, will ride calmly through the storms of life.

SIMILARITY HELPS

A few years ago my sister and I joined a travel group led by Dr. Charles Allen, an author and Methodist minister. Our destination was India, where we observed a young couple preparing for their wedding day. The family had arranged for them to be married. I have never really understood this system, but it has been working for the people of India for centuries. Perhaps they use the cultural similarities as a basis for the relationship. From that point they probably make a conscious effort to find love. In such a culture, choice precedes emotional involvement. Love can grow out of deliberate, persistent desire for success. If the mind follows the path of love, the heart should follow.

Research suggest that potential partners who wish to reduce risks inherent in an intimate relationship should assess the degree of similarity in their backgrounds. While there are certainly exceptions to this, the statistics seem relevant enough to examine.

For years, social scientists have been telling us that the more similar the cultural, social, educational, and religious background of a couple the greater the potential for intimacy. Romantic zest is not enough. The prospects of a harmonious relationship improve when two people share similarity of training, pace of living, ambitions, interests and taste. In most cases we tend to be drawn to people who have common interests. We say they *"speak our language."*

This research seems significant because couples in the gender community who have made their relationship work have cited similarity as a factor behind their success. Some women enjoy shopping with their husbands, and I know some who enjoy getting fashion advice. Wise crossdressers capture the charm of sharing these aspects of femininity with the women they love.

Apparently, the development of similar Venusian traits can bond the couple. Crossdressers have the potential to share femininity, which at times includes the allure of beautiful feminine clothing, as well as the boring task of cleaning the house or changing the baby.

PLANTS WITHOUT WATER

Archbishop Tutu said, *"We are made for love. If we do not love we will be like plants without water."* I believe we can be truly human only after we have shared intimacy with another person. Somewhere within us there is the ability to accept, care for, and feel warmly toward another person. In a modern world it is difficult to realize this, but when we open our hearts and our minds, it can happen. When we drop the barriers and let love in, we find true happiness. Even Jesus needed to be comforted. I remember the moving song which was sung by Mary Magdalene in the musical, **JESUS CHRIST SUPERSTAR:**

"Try not to get worried,
Try not to turn on to problems that upset you

Everything's all right, yes everything's fine.
And we want you to sleep well tonight.
Let the world turn without you tonight.
If we try we'll get by,
So forget all about us tonight."

NEXT STEP: ROMANTIC LOVE

"*Romantic love is like a mental illness, but it's a pleasurable*
one. It's a drug. It distorts reality, and that's the point of it."

Fran Lebowitz

Most of us have experienced the bliss of romantic love; the flutter of our hearts, and the feeling of total bliss. In our mind's eye, the presence of our lover could be equated to the sum total of the entire universe. These feelings are wonderful and glorious, and we never want the feelings to end, but while the passion of romantic love greatly enriches our lives, we need an anchor, a foundation if the feeling is to last. This anchor is intimacy, the kind of togetherness that motivates people to give freely of self and to willingly accept another person as he is.

While the word *intimacy* is a euphemism for sex, the sexual aspects of the relationship must be preceded by an emotional closeness and familiarity. The closeness must involve the inmost recesses of the heart. People with self-knowledge are best prepared emotionally to share life with another. Frequently, crossdressers have a blurred identity. Many struggle to define who and what they are.

Likewise, a woman who loves a crossdresser will feel a disequilibrium when the person she loves has not successfully communicated all aspects of his personality. Unfortunately, he can't share the truth about himself until he knows himself.

This describes the problem Jan and Ken faced. But in time intimacy and self-awareness opened their hearts. Because their relationship was characterized by an unselfish sharing of self, they were strong enough to overcome the obstacles frequently associated with crossdressing.

COMMIT TO INTIMACY

I am aware of the challenges faced by couples in the gender community. To make the relationships work, both persons must be willing to accept the other unconditionally. Here is a summary of my own commitment to intimacy. I will:

Share my mind and heart as freely as I share my body,
Be open about my fears, hopes, ideals, and dreams,
Develop a clear perspective of our relationship,
Understand the differences between how we express love,
Prepare for the risks,
Develop our common traits, interests, and goals,
Be an instrument of peace.

CHAPTER SIX
LOOKING FOR LOVE IN ALL THE WRONG PLACES

A popular song describes why some of us never find love. The lyrics say we are, "*Looking for love in all the wrong places.*" What does this mean? Where are we looking for love? Many are waiting for love to come to them through other people, but real love moves outward from the heart. The potential for love is within you.

Self-love comes slowly for Martians who feel like foreigners on their own planet. They desperately need to be validated by the persons close to them. Frequently, because of guilt and shame, they don't feel worthy of love. The problem relates to the egocentric nature of humanity. Too much of self-confidence seems to be dependent upon moment by moment gratification from others.

Once we have started to love ourselves, we have opened our hearts for the love from those near to us. We are not talking about the kind of self-love experienced by Narcissus, who looked into a pond, saw a reflection of himself, and fell very much in love with what he saw. From that time forward Narcissus found no room in his heart for anyone else. "*Shut out of his life, his lover faded away.*" The Narcissistic-kind of self-love wreaks destruction on relationships, for love is a mutual thing. Excessive self-love, at the expense of others, will deprive an individual of fulfillment.

The healthy kind of self-love is a self-appreciation necessary for good mental health. Self-doubt and self-rejection affect love relationships, because people tend to project their inner thoughts about self. In his book, **BORN FOR LOVE**, (Random House) Leo Busgaglia, Ph.D., describes the love of self, as well as the love for others, as something toward which we must continually work. But, according to Busgalia, we must forgive ourselves before our hearts are ready for love: "*You might forget your own telephone number,* *but you will have an unfailing memory for all the things you have done wrong, especially the past mistakes."*

SHARING LIFE WITH ANOTHER

If you believe you can not be happy without being involved in a relationship, you are showing symptoms of a person who has difficulty in relationships. This dependency upon love is a *set up* for a clinging, possessive attitude. Another person can not make you happy, make you feel good, or elevate your self-confidence. Ideally, you can move from the need for external approval to self-approval. Wanting to share a beautiful sunset with someone is natural. Feeling that there is no pleasure in the sunset when you are alone is not healthy. Unfortunately, our culture emphasizes external approval at the expense of internal harmony and honesty.

ELIMINATE THE NEGATIVES

We believe other people are making us unhappy when they do not love us in the way we want to be loved. When the wife of a crossdresser realizes her relationship varies significantly from the norm, as well as her expectations, she may feel resentment, anger, frustration, and fear. Some feel they are *swimming in a sea of negative thoughts and discouraging situations!*

These feelings are capable of causing unbelievable self-destruction. Since many inner feelings are stimulated by external forces, their impact can be handled or dissipated with effort. One thing is definite. Keeping negative thoughts around is detrimental to love, and will almost always harm any relationship. The wife may find the journey away from negative thoughts very much like *moving away from a victim role.* Bullough describes the scenario:

"... the characterization of wives as victims is not uncommon, and all of us have seen some 'doormat' wives who cook the food, scrub the floors, worry about the children, then go out to buy some beautiful article of feminine clothing which they give to their husbands. The husband accepts the part of the female role that

focuses upon leisure-time activities rather than on the drudgery of the role."

In a comprehensive research study, Bullough and Weinberg examined the importance of self-esteem for women. The findings of their study show a great variance in the levels of self-esteem among wives of crossdressers and a correlation between self-esteem and the acceptance of crossdressing, happiness, and internal control. Self-esteem seems to be the magic ingredient:

"Women with low self-esteem were more likely to feel they had failed in their role as wives. In addition, self-esteem and marital happiness were also correlated with the sense of internal control. Women who felt they controlled their own lives and did not feel buffeted by fate or controlled by other powerful persons not only had more self-esteem but also coped better with the stress of finding out about their husband's crossdressing activities."

If we look closely at the systematic test completed by these skilled researchers, we will see the need to build bridges from the shadows of pain back into our hearts through self-esteem. True feelings, including love and acceptance, begin within. We must learn to be true to our own identity before others can learn to relate to that identity. Self-approval precedes approval by others. This is a difficult concept for a Venusian whose husband has invaded her planet or for the Martian who has not come to terms with who he is. When a person finds little or no internal harmony, they can not expect to have a harmonious relationship with others. Don't demand love; create it!

Creating love involves looking inward and healing the psychological damage described by Robert Rowe, author of Bert and Lori:

"Like everyone who thinks of himself as a rebel or an outcast, I've suffered from self-imposed confusion, loneliness and doubt. Even now I still feel momentary twinges of conscience and shame whenever I even so much as think about putting on female clothing."

Once you have examined your heart, and resolved the issues found there, you will be ready to love yourself as well as accept the love of another person. Learn quickly the difference between a healthy self-love characterized by the absence of guilt and shame and the selfish, Narcissistic self-love exemplified by the person who looks at the world only from the view of personal gain. Crossdressers are being selfish when they say, "*My crossdressing hurts no one. My crossdressing is a need I must satisfy, come what may. Whatever the cost may be, I must have the opportunity to express my femininity. My wife and family will have to accept me as I am.*"

Crossdressing becomes very selfish when excessive amounts of the family budget are spent for additional feminine clothing while the wife and children go without. Selfishness is the opposite of true love, which is motivated by the desire to give. The irony is that selfish people really do not love themselves. They love no one.

Relationships tend to magnify inner conflicts. When we find peace within, we will usually find peace with others. We must come to grips with our own personal identities before others can know us. First, we must find a comfort zone of personal integrity. When this happens, we will diminish the value placed upon acceptance by those around us. We can search the world over a hundred times for acceptance, but it will come quickly once we accept ourselves. You may ask, "*Where do I look for love?*" Look first into your heart. Once you find love there, a new world opens up!

THE COMFORT ZONE

Even if it takes years to find a comfort zone with your own identity, you must keep searching. Acceptance from others will follow. At some time we may need to have the forgiveness of others, but of greater importance is the forgiveness we owe ourselves. Love is not about keeping old wounds open. Love is about healing wounds. It is about moving forward and learning from past mistakes. It is about getting on with life.

Coping may be little more than the ability to adjust to the mistakes of others, the courage to admit your own mistakes, and the confidence to march out of step when most other folks are hearing a different drummer. Nobody ever said life as a crossdresser would be easy. Society will make mistakes in its assessment of you because it does not have enough information to understand fully who you are. They see you as a person who is, *out of step with the rest of the world*. Your efforts to move forward will be plagued with false steps. You may become impatient with progress. It takes great confidence to march with poise if you are a Martian living a part of your life on Venus.

BASIC COPING SKILLS

We have all felt the burning pain experienced when people strike us with hurtful words, or when we feel that others have not fully accepted us. Most minorities, including crossdressers and their partners, may have experienced rejection, but there are a few basic skills which will help us cope:

1. *Learn to deal with problems successfully.*

2. *Define the problem and seek solutions, possibly with the help or input from others.*

3. *Handle or dissipate the fears and hurts of life in a constructive manner.*

4. *Recognize yourself as unique.*

5. *Realize your potential for true inner strength.*

6. *Develop the ability to move forward in spite of the lack of acceptance.*

7. *Keep learning from all experiences, both positive and negative.*

THE PAIN OF LONELINESS

During the process of finding self-acceptance, one can experience the feeling of being totally alone. Most crossdressers I have met tell about a lonely time in their lives. Many describe a *cosmic loneliness*. Love can get lost in the bigness of the universe.

Given the billions of people in the world, some wonder how their lives could possibly make a difference. But we live much of our lives one to another. You are important even within the greatness of the universe. You need never feel alone, but there are many times when you may feel there is no other person with similar needs.

There is a loneliness when we judge ourselves too harshly or when other people judge us. Many people are lonely because they build walls rather than bridges or others build walls of prejudice and ignorance. Assailed by social condemnation, we can feel completely unworthy.

In times of solitude it is good to affirm our own worth and direction, for the renewal of self makes us more ready to share life with others. We should capture the times of being alone for personal introspection. Times of solitude provide a fertile soil for personal growth and development. This is the time to reach within your heart where you will find truth, inspiration, and the flexibility to move gracefully through life. Robert Louis Stevenson challenged us, "M*ake the most of the best within.*"

SIX GIANT STEPS

There are advantages to being unique. If we take six giant steps we will continue to move forward:

First, set major goals in life, even if your goals are different from what others define for you. Begin right now, and get yourself a new target.

Second, start saying,"This which I have decided to do I can do." Say this until you believe it.

Third, do not be overly concerned about being unique. Novelty makes the world interesting.

Fourth, talk about your fears to somebody else. Just the expression of fears tends to overcome them.

Fifth, do not forget to laugh. Laugh both at yourself, at the situation, and at the world.

Sixth, remember there are other people who have the same

doubts, worries, and problems that you have. Be sympathetic, kind, and thoughtful of others.

As you continue the forward motion, remember to give:

1. *Forgiveness to those who do not understand your unique nature, and,*

2. *Tolerance to those who show displeasure with human differences.*

Even great people, such as Abraham Lincoln, had to work on the acceptance of self. We all know of Lincoln's accomplishments, and feel his worth helped make our country what it is today. But Lincoln had self-doubts that lasted throughout his life. He was dedicated to doing his best and spent his life trying to overcome negative feelings. You can overcome them as well. Once an individual has found contentment within his being, he is ready to reach out with unselfish love to another person. Happiness results from the attainment of what one considers good. Contentment is a peaceful kind of happiness in which one rests without desires, even though every wish may not have been gratified. George Grey Barnard, a noted sculptor, once said, "*Only through constant struggle do we gain or attain victory. The struggle in life is the important thing.*" Learning to accept ourselves is a life-long process which involves these actions:

1. *Remember that love does not come from external sources! Look first for love from within your own heart.*

2. *Take the responsibility for your own happiness.*

3. *Love yourself before you try to love another person.*

4. *Build a defense shield of confidence against harsh words or harsh treatment.*

5. *Think of love as an action more than a feeling. Love is what you do for yourself and others.*

6. *Think of yourself as complete. Another person will enhance who you are, but they can't make you what you are.*

7. Learn to be alone with yourself. If the experience of being alone is unpleasant others will not want to be with you either!

8. Growth is having a more complete experience with yourself. If you feel incomplete, you are not ready for love.

9. Become what you want others to be.

Look into the Bible to find a good definition of love. Ponder this idea as you read the truths found there. *"I am love. I will find love within my own being. Sharing my love with others is wonderful, for others make me a better version of myself."*

I Cor.13 says, *"Love rejoices in truth, Love does not behave unseemly and does not rejoice in iniquity. Love is kind and does not seek her own; is not puffed up, and is not easily provoked. Love lasts forever."*

CHAPTER
SEVEN
LEARNING TO
FACE
CONFLICT

*W*hen a couple says they have never had an argument, what they are actually saying is they have found successful ways of discussing their differences. They know how to have a creative *meeting of the minds*. Such people have looked deep into their psyche to find emotional stumbling blocks, and they know the ways society has molded thought processes. These couples know how to talk and how to make decisions fairly.

THE COMFORT ZONE

An observation of small children helps us understand how normal it is to vent feelings toward those persons you love the most. Children seem to save their worst behavior for their parents. The mother walks into the day care center, only to be greeted by whines rather than hugs. When the mother corrects the tears, there is a flood of bad behavior. The mother represents the child's comfort zone. When the child sees his mother, there is the freedom to dump everything that has been stored up all day.

The exact thing happens in love relationships. When we start to feel comfortable, we release some of our negative behaviors. We *permit* the other person to see another side of us. How many times have you come home from work tired and frustrated after putting up a front all day long. You smiled at the boss, tolerated the other employees, and painted on a veneer of pseudo professionalism for all the clients. When you finally got home, you dropped the fancy clothes and soaked for thirty minutes in a hot tub of suds. All the fake smiles are washed away with the bath water.

Suddenly, we find ourselves venting all our frustrations. We may scream at those we love the most. They become innocent victims in an inner war we have fought all day. We have held our feelings inside, and now we are ready to vent. Home is a safe place to be who we really are. It is difficult to keep the stresses inside indefinitely. Home is the place where we can dare to be real.

TRACK DOWN THE SOURCE OF THE PROBLEM

So how can we have a relationship in which we are free to be ourselves and at the same time respect the rights of the person we love? How can conflicts be resolved? Start by identifying who you are and what you are actually uptight about. It feels better to vent in the presence of the person we love, but the consequences may be unpleasant if we don't know the source of the feelings, and if we are not able to communicate the actual problem.

Next, we should identify what it will take to make us feel better. Martians handle stress by silence. Communicate your need for space to your partner. "*I am in the process of trying to understand myself better, and I need to sort some things out.*"

It is a good idea to follow this statement with some reassurance for the other person. It is natural for them to feel shut out and alone. "*Honey, I love you, and I promise to talk later. But right now it is difficult to help you understand all of this when I don't understand myself.*"

Silence has caused some problems between crossdressers and their partners. Numerous wives have told me they believe resolution is possible, but all they get is silence. John Gray has said, "*Quite often a man will suddenly stop talking and become silent. This was unheard of on Venus. At first a woman thinks the man is deaf. She thinks that maybe he doesn't hear what's being said and that is why he is not responding. The biggest challenge for women is correctly to interpret and support a man when he isn't talking.*"

It is usually each person's responsibility to respect a request for space, but in these cases the female partner is searching for answers and receiving none. She might need to verbalize an account of all the events of the day, including the discovery of a $400 charge from a department store for size 18 clothing.

TAKE RESPONSIBILITY FOR YOUR ACTIONS

An argument is a collision in which two chains of thought are derailed. Earl wanted to dress en femme and go out. Harriet wanted to visit with neighbors. Previously Harriet and Earl had accepted a dinner invitation with neighbors who knew nothing about the crossdressing. Obviously upset, Harriet expressed her frustration: *"That is the most outrageous thing! You are not thinking about my needs at all. I can't imagine how anyone could be so rude. We promised the neighbors!"* Earl was sorry and said so, and promised to talk with Harriet before making plans in the future.

The *ball is in Earl's court* in the matter of directing the conversation. The essential ingredients of Earl's response are:

1) *the apology,*

2) *the promise to do something about it, and*

3) *the tone of voice, which is kind enough to make the whole verbal exchange work.*

The person who becomes the kicking block for another person's frustration has more responsibility in the process of resolution. He may choose to perpetuate the problem by lashing back or attempt to be conciliatory. The complainer starts the verbal exchange, but it is the receiver who must make peace. This is a difficult concept but a very important one in relationships. Earl agreed with the complaint. *"Yes, this really is a mess. I will do my best to make it right. Your happiness is important to me. I am committed to you and our relationship!"* Earl's tone of voice gave reassurance to Harriet regarding the level of his commitment. He probably prevented a derailment on their collision course.

CONNECT WITH THE PAST

It is helpful to look into the things in your partner's background which contributed to unacceptable behavior. Childhood scars can remain with us into adulthood. When I was a child, I was taught to hold anger inside. Since this was not always possible, I found alternate ways to vent my frustrations and emotions. It is still not unusual for me to cry instead of scream! I no longer hold back my emotions and this is healthy not only for me but for all people who are important in my life. Earl probably remembers the years of hiding his gender identity, and feels the need to *push boundaries.* This does not excuse his lack of consideration for Harriet and the neighbors, but the knowledge of his past may help Harriet understand why Earl was not considerate of her needs.

Sometimes we are out of touch with the past and actually don't know why we are acting in a certain way. Realize that your partner may not have resolved all past issues either, and continue trying to connect with things in the past which may be causing the problems in the present.

When couples in the gender community experience disequilibrium, stereotypical social expectations are frequently the cause. Martians do this and don't do that. Venusians do this and don't do that. Couples clinging to these expectations become very uncomfortable when reality does not follow the cookbook that society imposes on the masses.

CONFLICT MANAGEMENT AND ANGER

There are numerous situations which may be the catalyst for anger. Some women hate shaven body parts on their partners. Others resent the limited choice of friends and find the circle narrowing around the people in the gender community. Many feel angry about conflict related to sex and intimacy. I doubt that anyone likes the anger which results from these scenarios.

The following set of questions can help us get into touch with the effect of the past upon our present. Ask these questions during a time when there is no stress and both of you feel like sharing.

1. *When you know I am angry with you, what are your thoughts and feelings?*

2. *Does my anger remind you of anyone in your past?*

3. *How do you want me to express my anger? What do you want me to do or say?*

4. *What would it take to make you feel safe when we disagree?*

In relationships it is important that each individual be able to sense problems the other has had and react appropriately. We all make mistakes in judgment from time to time. Watch your partner for signs that tension is building. Do your part to take appropriate action. The wise person knows the exact moment to purr like a kitten or roar like a lion. Or, in the case of a crossdresser, he knows when he should wear the pants and when it is OK to wear a dress.

Remember this important rule: *Even committed couples may disagree about some issues.* It is best to accept your true feelings rather than suppress them. Learn to respect your partner and her point of view by following these three actions:

1) *Negotiate,*

2) *Compromise, and*

3) *Take turns.*

Conflict happens, but our goal must be resolution. You may not yet agree about the direction the crossdressing will take in your relationship, but you can respect the views of each other, and try to keep the views separate from the love you share.

MAKE THE BEST OF BAD TIMES

Life is ten percent what you make it and ninety percent how you take it. No relationship is ever exempt from the harsh realities of life. It is the foolishness of bliss which leads us to believe sunny skies will forever shine over the love relationship. No one is ever excused from bad luck. While all seek a relationship characterized by joy and bliss, the real measure of success is how we handle life and thunderstorms. Turbulent periods will either destroy a relationship or polish and refine its beauty.

A rancher friend of mine explained this idea with an illustration. According to my friend, "*The difference between wild horses and wild mules can be seen when an adversary strikes. When a pack of wolves charge the horses, they will put their heads together in a tight, single body and kick the living daylight out of the wolves. If the mules are faced by the same adversary they will charge from all directions and kick the living daylights out of each other.*" Unfortunately, this example sounds a bit too much like the gender community. The story points up the need to unify in the face of conflict. Conflict is never as important as our reaction to it.

OBJECTIVE RATHER THAN SUBJECTIVE

When we have disappointments with the person we love, each person should be as objective as possible. Stick to the facts and keep value judgments out of it. Harriet felt disappointed because Earl did not respect a previous commitment. She was expecting an evening with her husband and their neighbors, and he decided to go out instead. Harriet made an appropriate objective statement. "*I do not like being left out of the decision making process. This makes me feel that I have no voice. Also I am not sure how to explain your absence to the neighbors They are expecting us to come over.*"

It is almost always wrong to impute feelings, motives or value judgments to another. A subjective statement would involve a value judgement or an opinion such as, "*I noticed you had no concern for my feelings. I can tell you really don't care for me any more! You care more for your crossdressing buddies than you do for me.*"

A more effective conversation would be one that showed empathy for Earl. "*You didn't call about your decision to go out dressed. I know you work very hard and look forward to getting dressed up. I'm sorry there is a conflict in our schedules. Since our previous plans involve the neighbors, I believe you should cancel the plans to go out dressed tonight. You know how I fear discovery by neighbors. I believe your absence will stir their curiosity.*"

Not only does this statement expresses concern for Earl's feelings and well being, but it proposes an alternate solution. Mutual giving and the desire to make each other happy enable love to overcome conflict. Someone said, "*Compromise is dividing the cake so that everyone thinks they got a big piece.*"

Somewhere between Earl's view and Harriet's there is a common ground. The real spirit of communication involves building upon the views of each other so that a *win-win* situation exists.

FIGHT BY THE RULES

Football games, governments, and even kindergarten classes have rules. Why not have rules for facing conflict with the person you love? Here are ten basic rules for conflict management:

Both of you must agree to discuss the conflict.

Realize the purpose of the discussion is to understand each other better and to apply knowledge about each other to the situation at hand. Ideally, the end result will be resolution.

Avoid hurtful words and accusations.

Speak softly.

Keep the problem between the two of you and attempt to avoid involving others in the conflict resolution process.

Mutually decide when the time is right to kiss and make up.

Put the issue behind and avoid retrieving it later once there is resolution.

Avoid casting blame.

Remember that love does not mean we like everything our partner does.

Act in a mature, responsible manner, working to find alternative solutions.

Listen to what your partner has to say, paraphrasing it to be sure you heard correctly.

Conflict resolution relates to accepting your relationship unconditionally. Our lives hold many opportunities for happiness. Arthur Rubinstein said, "*Most people ask for life on condition. Happiness can be felt only if you don't set conditions.*" This is the real secret for conflict resolution.

We live in a time when many people think of their needs first, even at the expense of others. Selfishness is rampant. The people we love are at the mercy of our demands when we say, "*If you loved me, you would do what I am asking you to do. You would not be opposed to my demands!*"

One of the first things couples must learn is to not make unrealistic demands upon each other, and never issue ultimatums. We must accept unconditionally the person we love.

Self-centered people tend to turn some very small issues into major problems. An angry crossdresser may say, "*I have to wait until after sunset to leave the house. I feel like a prisoner in my own home.*" What is happening here? It is obvious that some kind of compromise is needed, and much of the decision relates to the neighborhood and societal attitudes about crossdressing. This is a valid concern for persons who live in high rise complexes with a guard at the door or for couples with small children who have not been told about the dressing. It may be a concern for any couple. Some people have found it better to dress elsewhere, since wives frequently fear exposure in neighborhoods. The crossdresser's anger may be toward societal conventions, but he may take it out on his family. The process leading to a solution includes:

1. *Define the problem.*
2. *Propose a solution.*
3. *Pick one or more alternatives.*

DON'T CONFUSE LIKE AND LOVE

Be careful that very insignificant issues don't grow into major points of irritation. Usually, small problems have very simple solutions. Barbara hates having makeup stains on her best towels. In this case a workable compromise would be for Pete to have special towels to be used for makeup removal. When irritation occurs, it is important to keep the anger or frustration out of unimportant issues.

Love does not mean we like everything our partner does. Notice this conversation. "*I can't love you! You keep messing up my towels that way!*" In this conversation one person is equating the value of love with a $14.98 towel. Love can not be turned on and off like a faucet. It is ridiculous to say, "*I love you when you use your own towels, but I don't love you when mine get dirty.*"

It is possible to dislike dirty towels and love the person who got the towels dirty. I am one of those persons who enjoy pretty towels, but I can love my husband when he forgets to use his own. This is not to diminish the importance of my husband's *respecting* my request. I believe I deserve that courtesy.

You may be saying, "*What's the big deal! I really don't care what the towels look like!*" But you probably have your own set of trouble spots. Anytime Martians invade Venusian territory there will be problems that need attention. You may ask, "*Will we go out in public together? Can we really afford three wardrobes for the two of us? When, if ever, will we tell our parents, children, and friends? Do I have to agree to have sex with you when you are crossdressed? If so, to what extent will there be dressing, and how will we balance the sex with the masculine and feminine persona? Will we actively participate in organizations? How often should the dressing occur? Why doesn't he honor my 'Keep Away Venusian' signs! There are times I don't want the femme side around!*"

Love can be the most fulfilling aspect of life, but enduring love will not be a reality until we love the person more than we dislike irritating actions. We must not confuse the person with the action. The two must remain separate in our minds. I have done extensive consulting with crossdressers and their families and have found negotiation within the boundaries of love to be especially important. All those involved must learn to keep the issue of clothing from threatening the love on which the relationship is based. We can love people in male clothing, female clothing, or no clothing. We can love the person even when we don't like the clothing. It really doesn't matter. Some people have said, "*It is possible to reject the dressing and continue to love the person doing the dressing.*" I wonder if this is true. When a wife rejects her husband's desire for feminine expression, she rejects a portion of who he is. The key point here is to realize the husband is the same man she married regardless of what he is wearing. Clothes do not turn a man into a woman.

Look at your life tapes and your present as you attempt to understand the problem. Here is a system which will help you track down negative feelings:

1. *Identify the actions we find upsetting.*
2. *Toss out our previous ideas about the activity.*
3. *Hold tenaciously to the love for the person who does the activity.*
4. *Keep your mind open to options as you work through the problem.*

Shakespeare said, "*There is nothing either good or bad, except thinking makes it so.*" Place into your mental balance the negative value of the problem and weigh it against the value of the relationship. On which side does the scale fall? Do you want to preserve the relationship with your partner? How important are her needs? Are you willing to make sacrifices or do you expect your wife/partner to make all the sacrifices?

Why is the choice of clothing so important? The problem relates to our *tapes* which may be different from those of our partner. We simply do not see things the same. Love is a process we have learned during our lives. When two people merge their lives, it follows logically that neither can get his way all the time. We are familiar with the expression, *give and take*. In reality there must be more *give* than *take*. Differences may lead to arguments, suffering, and unhappiness. There must be compromise, appropriate boundaries, and sharing. Open discussions about what our likes and needs are is important. Try to maintain balance as you structure a plan everyone can live with.

DON'T QUIT

Building a good life and developing a strong relationship requires persistence. Things will go wrong. Adjustments must be made; but if you are committed to the relationship, you will keep trying! Often the goal is nearer than it seems.

When things go wrong as they sometimes will,

When the road you are trudging seems all uphill,

When the funds are low and the debts are high,

You want to smile, but you have to sigh,

When care is pressing you down a bit,

Rest if you must, but please don't quit!

Life is strange with its twists and turns,

But many a failure can be turned about.

You can win , but you must stick it out!

Don't give up when

The pace seems slow.

You might succeed with one more blow.

Often the good is closer than you think.

But if you give up,

You wont capture the victor's cup!

Some people learn too late

How close they were to the golden crown.

Success is failure turned inside out.

It is the silver tint of a cloud of doubt.

You never can tell how close you are.

Success may be close when it seems afar.

So stick to the fight when you're hardest hit.

It's when things seem bad that you mustn't quit.

Author unknown.

WHEN WE DON'T SEE EYE TO EYE

There is a story told about two knights who met on a path near the castle. They both saw a shield which had been tied to a tree nearby. The first knight asked, "*Whose kingdom owns the white shield?*" The second knight said, "*You are blind and you are also very dumb. That shield is as black as midnight.*" The first knight was quick to scream back, "*What do you think I am a blind fool or a stupid fool?*" At that moment both knights drew their swords and began to brutally attack each other.

Just then a third knight approached the scene and asked why the two of them were about to kill each other. After an explanation, the third knight asked that the two change places to see if a different vantage point would also change their view. When the positions were changed the two knights could clearly see the vantage point of the other. Rather than continue the battle, they became friends and rode off into the sunset together.

When we are in a relationship with another person, we will not always see things the same. Frequently, there will be truth on both sides. We need to stop and look carefully at the other person's viewpoint. This takes patience and wisdom. This is so difficult because we have held many of our convictions for most of our lives. To strip them away is almost like sacrificing a part of our identity. When one partner's ideas seem unimportant to the other, it is interpreted as an insult to their true identity. And out come the swords.

One door and only one
And yet the sides are two
I am on the inside.
On what side are you?

A DOZEN AND A HALF WAYS TO HANDLE CONFLICT

1. *Find a comfort zone where you can be yourself.*

2. *Communicate how you like to handle stress.*

3. *Take responsibility for your actions.*

4. *Connect with the past and stop letting it have a negative affect on your present.*

5. *Learn to handle anger.*

6. *Be sensitive to your lover's needs.*

7. *Make the best of bad situations.*

8. *Stay objective.*

9. *Fight by the rules.*

10. *Keep your wishes realistic.*

11. *Forget about ultimatums.*

12. *Keep little issues insignificant.*

13. *Learn to identify the source of negative thoughts.*

14. *Learn to handle disappointments.*

15. *Strive to be mature.*

16. *Accept your partner unconditionally.*

17. *Be persistent in your effort to make your relationship work.*

18. *Remember, there are two sides to every story.*

Pull together! It is impossible to make any progress rowing your boat in two directions at the same time

Venusians are subjective and idealistic. Venusians long for security and love.

Martians are objective and realistic. Martians are willing to take risks and desire respect.

Why not give up the stereotypes and seek the better qualities of Mars and Venus? Balance and integration improve life on Planet Earth!

CHAPTER EIGHT
MAKING
A
COMMITMENT

"Hearts are not had as a gift,
But hearts are earned by those
That are not entirely beautiful."
From William Butler Yeats, **A Prayer For My Daughter**

*I*n a perfect world filled with perfect people it would be easy to make a commitment to love, honor, and cherish. But as Yeats has written, people are never entirely perfect or beautiful. Perfection is a dream, a fantasy, with no guarantee of bliss.

Bob pondered issues related to commitment. *"I have met some one who may be 'the girl' for me. How do I know the right time to discuss my femme side? How do I know she is a person who can accept this part of me? I realize the gamble here. Part of me wants to hide the truth from her, but this doesn't seem fair. I'll admit that the thought of losing her because of my Venusian side scares me to death! I am so in love with her! I know I will accept her unconditionally, but I am less sure of her ability to accept the cross-dressing. Asking her to accept a life-style so unique, and so different from the norm, seems like asking her to take a giant leap."*

BE PREPARED

After talking with Bob for a while, I felt the time was right for him to share the truth with Patricia, the woman he had been dating for seven months. First, however, I encouraged him to take another look at himself by answering some critical questions as honestly as possible. Bob related the set of questions to his experience as a

Boy Scout. "*Our leader told us to be prepared.*" With that memory in mind Bob focused on my questions:

Have you accepted yourself?

Do you have a clear understanding of the role sex and gender play in your life?

If there are children involved, have you thought about how your crossdressing will affect them?

Is the woman you love secure and self-confident?

Have you been successful in handling other conflicts within your relationship?

Is your relationship based upon honesty and trust?

Do you have a solid information and support system in place including literature and other couples who have successfully integrated crossdressing into a love relationship?

Are you prepared to put your own needs on hold indefinitely?

Are you patient enough to wait for her adjustment?

Are you aware that the issue of crossdressing will have an impact upon your relationship, and sometimes the results will be out of your control?

Since life is seldom about total bliss and human differences are a way of life, it behooves us to make a commitment only when we possess the skills to resolve problems, constructively, as Bob has done. Life is about struggle, compromise, giving, and sharing. Crossdressers are certainly guaranteed a unique set of challenges. Whether or not we are ready to make a lasting commitment depends upon our ability to utilize the skills of constructive problem solving. We must practice patience, determination, and resilience.

Too many people prefer to wait for utopia rather than commit the effort to improve their relationships. They are like the man who stands on the bank and condemns the swirling white waters below. While at the same time, constructive men are busy building dams to control the angry water. If we prepare well for life commitments, they can enrich lives, but commitments do require application of intellect, determination, and creative energy. When we fail to fulfil a commitment, we have created a situation of agony, because people need others. Broken commitments will sacrifice human well-being, and the by-products are alienation, broken promises and ultimately a broken trust. This is why divorce is so messy. It is like having the security blanket removed, and the harsh elements of life are at liberty to pound down like a ferocious storm. Make commitments carefully for loneliness lurks around the altar.

UNDERSTAND THE RISKS

Crossdressers have only to look around the community to find evidence of the risks involved. Many relationships end because some people are afraid or unwilling to commit all aspects of their lives to the one they love. Self-interest and selfishness prevent the integration of life with another. There is no desire to compromise. The words *my, mine, I and me* have more melodious sounds than *us, we, our and ours.*

Why is there so much reluctance to give? To many cross-dressers, commitment is synonymous with pain. And why is this? Try as I might, I can't get rid of the picture of the toddler's temper tantrum. The scenario goes like this:

Husband, *"I want to dress every day."*

Wife, *"I am not sure this is practical. I am afraid of the consequences of exposure, and we should think about the children."*

Husband, *"I want to take hormones to grow breasts and feel more like a woman."*

Wife, *"But what about the side-effects, especially on your health and on our sex-life?"*

Husband, *"I feel pain!"*

The psychological and emotional need to transcend Venus and Mars adds a new layer of risk and pain to the formula. Both partners feel the sting. Crossdressing is a unique behavior, but the couples who are motivated to make it work have been very successful. There are no guidelines other than the one that says, *"Both of you must work on it!"*

DECIDING THE LEVEL OF COMMITMENT

While some relationships have survived a lack of intense commitment, the individuals usually find fulfillment elsewhere. If, for example, both the man and woman are in power positions on the job, each person may discover that careers consume most of their energy. Such couples may not experience the level of satisfaction and closeness with each other.

A similar scenario occurs when crossdressers decide to commit huge amounts of time to their Venusian traits. This is complicated when their wives or partners do not want to participate in crossdressing. When crossdressers consume excessive energy for the femme side, there may be little left for the partner. The woman begins to feel *replaced* and less committed. Couples must address these concerns, because alienation may be the end result.

Both persons must agree to share their commitment with careers, crossdressing, or other valued aspects of their lives. Problems arise when one partner is more committed to the relationship than the other. For example, a very successful man may want his wife to stay at home, be a wife and mother, and experience success vicariously through his career. Some women are able to do this, but others cannot. In the same way, some wives want their husband to stop crossdressing. Since there is no *cure*, ending the crossdressing is not a viable option, even if the wife or partner is adamant. Compromise, however, is possible.

In this situation *honesty* is of the utmost importance. Define what you want out of the relationship and out of your life. How far do you want the commitment to go? What are you willing to share? If the two of you can agree on a low commitment profile and can both be happy with it, your relationship can work. The important thing is that you follow through on what you promised, so that trust can remain strong.

I believe the degree to which we open up to another person is equal to our *acceptance of vulnerability*. Fortunately, the gift of self carries with it feelings of joy and a sense of well-being. Couples I know who have been successful at integrating crossdressing into their relationships feel more togetherness than other couples, and a greater joy.

Gloria Steinem once explained the risks of relationships in this way: *"Someone once asked me why women don't gamble as much as men do, and I gave a common-sense reply that we did not have as much money. That was a true but incomplete answer. In fact, for women, the total instinct for gambling is satisfied by marriage."*

Both the crossdresser and their partners, take risks in the name of selfishness. Men, for the most part, are more willing to take risks by going out in public or telling too many people about the crossdressing. This is a *Martian* thing. I would challenge the crossdresser to take another step toward Venus. *Temper risks with security and peace of mind for the woman he loves and for himself. Gambles* in other areas of life are less difficult, because they are less emotional. We make commitments to banks when we hand over our money for safe keeping. When necessary, we commit ourselves to a doctor for care of our bodies. We show that we are committed to an organization by paying our dues, attending meetings, and participating in the work.

OTHER CONSIDERATIONS

When the risk involves our emotional *bank* we are far less willing to commit. Crossdressing involves the emotions as well as personal identity. Answer these critical questions before making a commitment:

1. *Do I really want to share my time?*
2. *Am I willing to invest my energy?*
3. *What are my limits?*
4. *To what degree do I contribute to the other person's sense of well-being?*
5. *What do I plan to bring into the relationship, and what do I expect to get out of it?*
6. *How much am I willing to compromise my wants to meet her needs?*

After thinking about these questions, discuss them with your partner. Determine what your needs are. Be equally concerned about how well you meet the needs of the person you love. Luck has a peculiar habit of favoring those who don't depend upon it. In the process of making a commitment, it is best to leave little to chance. If you prepare well for a commitment, good luck will probably follow .

ARE WE THERE YET?

On road trips children often ask, "*Are we there yet?*" A journey seems long and tedious for a child. In the same way a journey toward commitment may also be stressful. If you are already married but have not made the quality commitment described here, you are over-due. Let these guidelines direct your path, and make the sacrifices needed to get there. If you have not shared cross-dressing with your partner, try very hard to lay the groundwork for sharing all aspects of your personality with the person you love.

Persons who are not in a serious relationship may be eager to find a person among the billions of people in the world who is suited to them. Sometimes they may grow weary of the search. When they find Mr. or Miss Right, they must realize this is not the only such person in the world who is compatible with them. Such an attitude sets up a dependency, a feeling of, "*I had better hang on for dear life, because if I lose this one my whole life is down the drain!*" There is no need for such desperation.

You are ready for a commitment if you have found a person who reflects your own level of self-actualization. You should share similar goals and aspirations. In addition recognize the parts of each other that are lovable and the other parts which are forgivable. Each partner must play the role of helper when problem areas arise. Learn to assist rather than criticize. Then your lives will become a celebration of mutual actualization. There is no *I* in the word *teamwork,* and *cooperation* is based upon the concept of *we* rather than *me.* Crossdressing does not close the door to happiness. As John Barrymore said, *"Happiness sneaks in through a door you didn't know you left open."* Open the door. You may be pleasantly surprised! But you will need to commit to success. Stopping at third base adds nothing to the score! The team player will need to move forward to home base.

MAKING THE COMMITMENT

Praised by the troubadours of the thirteenth century, romantic love figured in marriage around the eighteenth century; but, even then, it was a luxury afforded only by the wealthy, well-educated people of the time. Parents were active supervisors and were expected to bless the marriage contract which clearly delineated the roles of each person. The norm today is a commitment based upon human interaction. Psychological compatibility has become more important. Love and personal happiness are the motives.

I can remember the first step my husband and I took in the direction of making the commitment we enjoy. The commitment began to form the January evening when we met. I was the organizer for an excursion to San Antonio for a Christian singles' convention. He came to my home to get more information about the trip. The expected time for this type of call is about 20 minutes. That night we found ourselves deep in conversation until the wee hours. Both of us recall how much we enjoyed the evening and how relaxed we felt. Time passed quickly. Neither of us could realize how it got late so soon. We had difficulty remembering ever being strangers.

As time passed we discovered many common interests. We also discovered personal faults, but we knew the joys shared would compensate for the weaknesses. In most cases we saw life from the same vantage point. Although we didn't always agree, there was a tolerance, because the common factors outweighed differences. Understanding took over where similarities stopped. We enjoyed spending our time together, because we were suited to helping each other grow. Soon we discovered that teamwork overcame selfishness. The secret of pooling attributes had compensated for weaknesses. We were in love!

THE PROCESS

In relationships that transcend Venus and Mars, partners must make commitments *slowly and very carefully*. Guilt and low self-esteem must be eliminated. There is no real universal criterion for making commitments, especially in the gender community. It is more a matter of being in touch with your own feelings and the feelings of the other person. Discuss problems and burdens, and share private thoughts. In time compatibility or a lack of it, will be evident. Since there are no real guidelines, most couples must struggle forward by trial and error. Although mistakes are a fact of life, it helps to learn to trust your feelings and the feelings of your partner, even when life is not smooth. You will be hurt sometimes; but, even then, put up an antenna which will help you know when your lover has been in pain. Learn to talk through problems calmly and compassionately. Be both forgiving and understanding.

We live in a time when *free love* is very dangerous. It was once easy to have a *one night stand* without being in love or making a commitment. Today we are virtually compelled to define love in terms of commitment. This makes it imperative that we understand what it means to share a life with another.

There are those who say, "*Commit to one person? No way! I don't want to lose my independence.*" If the truth be known, we are all dependent upon others in varying degrees. As you move toward a commitment, remember to keep your true identity. Do not permit your unique personality to disintegrate. It is difficult to be truly happy as a shadow of yourself.

THE FEAR FACTOR

"Everything we do in life is based upon fear, especially love," wrote Mel Brooks. Some people believe commitment gets a little scary because another individual becomes one of the most important aspects of our life. To some this feels like a loss of power. Some crossdressers are in love with the femme side and fear losing *her* to another woman. Others fear that love can not last forever. Still others see love as an affair of short spasms. If these spasms are pleasant, the love lasts; but if they are disappointing, it may die. Persons in the last category need to brush up on coping skills.

Socrates also saw some risks. *"By all means marry; if you get a good wife, you'll be happy. If you get a bad one you will become a philosopher."* Lily Tomlin appeared to be thinking along the same lines when she said, *"If love is the answer, will you rephrase the question?"* I place a greater value on love and believe if we refuse *to go out on a limb* we will never get to where the fruit is.

MOVE TOWARD INTEGRATION

The literal meaning of integration is, *"To make into a whole, and to make complete."* I wonder if Lilly Tomlin has experienced the joy of a relationship characterized by harmony and love. After reading these quotes, I am reminded of an old saying that more closely matches my own attitude about commitment: *"Nothing ventured, nothing gained."* We should not listen to the pessimists of the world lest we enter relationships expecting to lose, creating a self-fulfilling prophesy. A commitment to success will encourage us to develop strong relationships. When we make a commitment, a part of self is integrated into the life of another person. Ideally, a satisfaction follows as we move in the direction of *we* as opposed to *me*. Three warnings:

1. *Don't lose yourself;*

2. *Share yourself, and*

3. *Hold on to a personal identity.*

Mutual sharing is an experience which committed lovers can enjoy. I have talked with many couples who have enjoyed a higher level of commitment, and they know a wonderful sense of pleasure which can be found in no other way.

In the early part of a relationship men tend to hold tenaciously to their personal space. This is a trait of Martians. Crossdressers will improve as they move closer to Venus, for the focus of Venusians is upon nurturing and giving of self to others....reaching beyond self to others.

When I first met my husband, he was a *free spirit* who enjoyed making his own decisions, moving in his own space, and doing and saying exactly what he wanted. I can remember the fear he had of commitments, because his previous experience in his first marriage had been painful. Even on our wedding day he felt an uneasiness. A few months after we were married I began to think of him as a soaring bird who charts his own course from day to day.

The following poem expressed my perceptions of the one who ultimately returned to the *nest*.

FREE SPIRIT

With wings outstretched he soars,
High into the sky so blue,
With only the clouds to obstruct his view.
He feels the breeze against his wing,
As a melody of songs he starts to sing.
He is free to move and free to fly.
Soaring upward toward heaven,
He brushes the sky.
But sometimes a storm cloud darkens the blue,
A turbulence stirs the morning dew,
And he must struggle to gain more height.
Dust and wind obscure his view
At evening time,
As the sun glistens so sublime,
He finds his way, to rest at home,
A blanket of sky, a protective dome,
It's home at last for peace and love.

Only after the bruises started to heal, and the quiet of home was converted into a peaceful heart, did he make a real commitment. In retrospect I believe I was right to allow him to *fly freely* for a while. He rarely needs to be a *free spirit* any more. Today he is no longer afraid of our commitment, and is the first to advocate this type of relationship. One of his favorite songs says, "*You are the wind beneath my sail.*" Our home is his *refuge*. He lives for the time we can spend together and the enjoyment of our home and the many friends we have made in our seventeen years of marriage.

We perceive freedom to be a jealous mistress. To enjoy her we must reject her ancient competitor, possession. Freedom will not accept a divided allegiance. Our relationship is best understood with a drawing of two overlapping circles. We each enjoy a part of life together, the space overlapping, and an individuality separate and apart from the relationship. This is true freedom!

We understand the words of Don Juan:

"It was not love for woman that delivered me into her hands; it was fatigue and exhaustion.

When I was a child, and bruised my head on a stone, I ran to the nearest woman and cried away my pain against her apron.

When I grew up, and bruised my soul against the brutalities with which I had to strive, I did again just what I had done as a child."

Hopefully, Don Juan was not saying that when Martians move into the figurative troubled waters between Venus and Mars, they must find solace in the femme persona. Nor is he saying women must assume a mother role, and men only need a woman because they still crave mothering. It does say that the security of a relationship relates to a sincere concern for the welfare of each other. Warm affection, is an antidote for alienation and loneliness.

THE QUALITY COMMITMENT

The literal meaning of commit is, *"to hand over for safe keeping."* People will not *"hand over"* their lives to another person until there is trust, confidence, a feeling of safety and security.

Lasting commitments share some common factors. First, is *concern for each other*. The unity of the two persons makes selfishness yield to *mutuality*. In the musical, **MY FAIR LADY**, Lerner and Loewe imply that Professor Higgins will not marry Eliza. Not wanting a lasting commitment, Higgins appeared concerned primarily for his own well-being. In the final scene he turns to Eliza and snaps, "*Eliza, where the devil are my slippers?*" While Higgins didn't want to commit any part of himself, he expected her to serve his selfish whims. Surely commitment is stronger than the "*fetch dog scenario*" played here by Eliza. In the stage version, **PYGMALION**, the professor admitted, "*I've grown accustomed to your face, your smile, and your appearance, and I rather like them, but I can do without anybody. I have my own soul, my own spark of fire.*" It seems obvious that Higgins was not ready for commitment.

Higgin's world revolved around himself, and the path of rotation was too small to bring another person in. What is involved in making a commitment? The decision to share life with another becomes easier when the individuals care deeply for each other. *Self-confidence* is the foundation. It is very difficult to care for the needs of another when one is still struggling for *self-esteem*.

Deep introspection must occur in ourselves before we can help fill the voids of another person. *Warm affection*, consistently demonstrated by each partner towards the other, is an antidote for alienation and loneliness. There must be *mutual understanding* derived from talking things out. It is important to give as well as receive. *Communication*, both verbal and nonverbal, enables understanding to develop. Ultimately this will lead to a committed relationship if you are right for each other. If, on the other hand, the chemistry is not there, you will discover commitment is not the right choice. Some would say, "*Better late than never.*"

Open, honest *communication* is vital. In typical gender roles it is the Venusian who wants to talk things through. Martians would rather go to what Gray calls *The Cave* to think things through. This may be an area in which crossdressers, who have large feminine components, would be better with one foot in Venus as expressed by my short verse:

CHATTING, a trait from Venus.
Guys, please don't balk!
TALK.

THE MOTIVATION

What motivates a person to move beyond the Higgin's mentality? As my husband and I approached the time to make a commitment we considered *sincerity* vital. When the person we love makes mistakes, falls short of expectations, or becomes negligent, it is easy to forgive when each person has been sincere. If my husband is doing his best, I am inclined to walk that extra mile. *Sincerity* is one of the prerequisites to love and lasting commitments.

Women frequently list *affection* as the most important aspect of a love relationship and lasting commitments. Women demonstrate love with gestures, smiles, and tenderness, and they want their partners to show affection as well. Simeon Porter realized the importance of affection when he said, "*The world of ideas is first arranged in five broad categories of abstract relations. These are space, matter, intellect, volition, and affection.*"

People are more inclined to make a commitment when there is *cooperation and teamwork.* Teamwork in a relationship is like teamwork in a baseball game. You can't win all by yourself nor can your partner win all alone. There is value in working together. The direction the commitment moves must be mutually decided, and it can take any form the couple agree upon. When plotting your course with each other, it is important to:

Find a person whose interests, values, and goals are similar to yours and be sure you like to be with the person you are contemplating as your life partner.

Mutually decide upon the nature and manifestation of the commitment.

Be willing to give up a part of self to gain the feeling of togetherness.

Give the commitment time to mature.

Be willing to accept your partner's imperfection.

Prepare for human differences.

Understand the risks involved in relationships.

Commit your life to a person who shares your own self-actualization.

Understand the loneliness which may follow when the commitment does not work out.

Follow these guide lines for commitment, and remember the secret to happiness is not only what you give or receive but what you share with another person.

" First comes love
Then comes marriage
Then comes baby in a baby carriage.

When children are a part of the picture, the
utmost is called for on the part of both par-
ents. Neither parent can allow his or her
own needs to impinge upon the children's
need for a loving, stable environment."

From *Children and Crossdressing: Sailing an*
Uncharted Sea by Frances and Jane Ellen Fairfax.

CHAPTER NINE
WHAT ABOUT
THE
CHILDREN

*O*ne of the most difficult questions faced by couples in the gender community relates to *how* crossdressing should be introduced to children or *if* the children should be told. There are probably as many answers to these question as there are children involved. There are many variables and no simple answers. The following story describes an experience of two young women who discovered, quite by accident, that their father is a crossdresser. After moving the full cycle from disbelief to acceptance, one of the girls summed up her feelings. *"The hardest battle a human can fight is to be himself in a world which attempts to control the definitions of reality and stereotypical normalcy."* Look closely at their account, and you will see the almost ideal scenario.

Our names are Isabelle and Louise. We grew up in Louisiana, surrounded by hot bayous and crawfish in the happiest family ever. As children we had it made! Best friends lived next door, dolls and match box cars filled our room, and Mom and Dad were always there for us. We remember Mom as being intelligent, loving, and beautiful and Dad as being wise, yet silly. He told us stories about helicopters and oil rigs and always included examples which led us in the direction of independence and wisdom. He taught us to look out for ourselves and be careful with the decisions we made. Our parents were strict with rules, but they helped us see the world as a kaleidoscope. We learned to recognize and respect the differences in people. Our parents were neither racist nor sexist, so by their example we came to look at the world with an open mind. In time we formulated a value system and our own set of beliefs .

Our family moved to North Carolina during middle school years when Dad changed jobs. Time was divided between school, playing musical instruments and doing homework. Dad had a workshop in the back yard and spent a lot of time there fixing everything, from cars to televisions. Mom was at home a lot after teaching. She loved to keep a garden filled with flowers and vegetables. On weekends the family took long bike rides and enjoyed supper off the grill with friends. As sisters, we had our usual teenage fights about staying out late or going somewhere with friends; but, basically, we got along well because we were both girls and we were close to the same age. Each of us enjoyed helping the other with problems.

Childhood passed quickly! We were teens before anyone could realize where the years had gone! In high school we were involved in many activities. We joined clubs, toured Europe and went on school trips. Soon we were projecting our thoughts toward the future. Our father began to teach us about finances and how to succeed in business. Mom helped us with school work and the problems all young people face. Our minds were like rubber bands: stretching to fathom the world and its complicated components. Life seemed blissful. We were lucky to have a family that was supportive. We actually thought our family fit the typical American prototype and believed we fit the social norm perfectly.

One day this notion changed dramatically! Isabelle found a pair of sunglasses in the car and thought that Dad might be having an affair, because she did not recognize them. A greater shock followed! She found Dad dressed up as a woman. Louise found wigs and purses in Dad's closet and, knowing Dad, suspected them to be some joke or romantic game. We talked to each other and found out that our stories appeared to be related.

Since we were taught to be open and honest, it seemed best to talk to him about what we had discovered. At that time we were introduced to the fascinating world of crossdressing. He told us that he liked dressing up because it was fun and helped him relax. Neither of us could understand at first, because it seemed strange, and wrong. From our point of view having to get dressed up was a hassle. We were bored with curling hair and applying make up. We got tired of spending two hours just to look pretty. The dresses and panty hose were uncomfortable. It was difficult to understand how they made him feel relaxed. We questioned my Mom's opinion of it and wondered how she could feel comfortable. We found out that she wasn't, at first. It took six months for her to totally understand the reasoning behind our dad's Venusian traits.

Something strange happened. Our concept of reality changed and our family dynamics began to expand to include a new perception of what a father can be. In time we began to comprehend the variance within the world. A world that was previously black or white was tinted with shades of gray. We no longer assumed that Fred Astaire wears the top hat and Ginger Rogers wears the long, lovely gowns. Costumes are just costumes and a person's personality can prevail even when society falls short of the ideal.

WHAT IS THE ANSWER? DO WE TELL THE CHILDREN?

Recently, a crossdresser asked Jane Ellen Fairfax if he should tell his 11 year old son about his gender preference. Jane's response is summarized below. Read carefully, for Jane's answer presents some things to consider when reaching a decision. The choice of whether, when, how, and why children should or should not be told is highly personal. Each child, and each family, is different and has different needs.

The first principle about telling the children of your gender gift is that there is no principle. To our knowledge, no one has done prospective studies on the consequences of telling, or not telling, children. It does not appear that telling children about crossdressing encourages them to take up the practice. For many years, we have worked with families struggling with this issue. A few observations have occurred we would like to share.

The very worst time to tell a child is adolescence. When a child is struggling with his own emerging sexuality and gender expression, the last thing he needs is to have a parent's sex and gender issues thrust on him. If you decide to tell your child, you should consider doing so very soon. At 11, puberty is just around the corner.

Most people decide to tell their children on a need-to-know basis. If you are going to work extensively in the community, and be out and about, it is probably best to tell your child. In this way, you will have control over what he is told, and how. If someone else tells him first, you will have not only the crossdressing issue, but also the thornier issue of trust to deal with.

Much of the child's reaction depends on whether the parents present a united front. If your wife is encouraging and supportive, this factor will work for you in a big way. Children want first the secure knowledge that any given factor will not disturb the stability of their family. When the father tells them about the crossdressing, their first thought will be, *"What does Mom think about this?"*

You may be surprised if you get some noncommittal reaction from the child. The news may be overwhelming. You should not push too hard, but you should re-expose him in low doses so that he does not go into denial. If he has another supportive relative with whom to talk over these issues, that is all to the good. How the child does in the long run will depend on the fruits crossdressing bears in his life. He will need his father for a masculine role model. Crossdressing should not interfere with his social life. The cross-dresser's desire to be everything he is should not prevent the child from bringing his peers home. Nor should the crossdresser try to force his values on his children's friends.

If you have any security considerations, we would advise meeting them by stressing to your child the impropriety of telling other people your business. Children do not tell other people what Daddy makes or what he occasionally likes to wear.

Love is the most important element. When children get plenty of this commodity, they do not tend to forget the love because of their dad's crossdressing. As always, you do well to stress self-expression rather than the superficial clothing. An 11 year-old child may or may not have fears that he will lose you as a father. If he does, reassure him if you can truthfully do so. You are his father, regardless of what you are wearing.

For further information about children's issues write to:

Tri-Ess International
8880 Bellaire Boulevard, B2- Suite 104
Houston, Texas 77036-4621
E-mail: jeftris@ aol.com
Web site: http://www.tri-ess.com

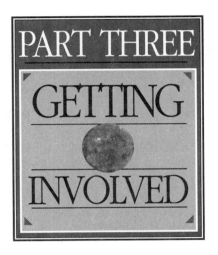

PART THREE

GETTING

INVOLVED

At some point couples within the gender community feel a need for companionship with people who share similar interests and face similar challenges. Unfortunately, I have known only a few who felt prepared to move out of the safe confines of their home and into support group activities.

At first the thoughts of meeting other crossdressers and their wives or partners is frightening; but when individuals meet the challenge, there is a new beginning, with opportunities for personal growth and a more complete life. The people who take the giant step out frequently discover this to be the beginning point of walking the golden mile toward self-actualization and fulfillment as a couple.

CHAPTER TEN
PRISCILLA, QUEEN OF THE SEAS

*T*he open hand holds more love than the closed fist. We all know this; but when Martians start acting like Venusians, and crossdressing is introduced within a marriage or committed relationship, most of us are inclined to react less than favorably. Staying within the norm seems more comfortable for most people. Recently, I met a group of women who chose to open their hearts to love rather than retaliation. The demonstration of their love had a far-reaching effect for their relationships, and to 1400 people who observed the demonstration of their love .

It all began when these women joined their husbands on the Seventh Annual **DIGNITY CRUISE** to Bermuda in September, 1996. Each woman felt her husband deserved an opportunity to enjoy fine dining and pampered service, shopping and sightseeing while fully dressed as a woman. Each woman knew the emotional pleasure her husband would experience when pictures were made with the captain of a luxury cruise ship, when waiters in tuxedos helped with her chair, and when the doormen called her "*Lady*". It was a dream come true. The experience was the ultimate validation!

Each woman knew the potential enrichment for her own relationship. What she did not expect was the wave of acceptance from the other passengers on board and the most tremendous outreach opportunity of their lives. The 1400 passengers will never forget meeting our group.

Acceptance was not evident on the first day. In fact most people didn't notice we were there. Perhaps it was because the other passengers were feeling the ultimate pleasure for themselves. They were too caught up in the atmosphere to notice a small group of very tall women. A few may have wondered if the Canadian

Women's National Basketball Team was on board.

We began to be noticed soon after Carol, Babs, Jody and Char bought a horse to be entered in the races later in the week. I use the word, *horse* loosely, since she was only a stick pony without even a hint of a costume. Very soon the pony had a name, **PRISCILLA, QUEEN OF THE SEAS**, which she wore proudly wherever she went, and she went everywhere! Shortly thereafter, she also had a costume, and what a costume it was! Everyone noticed the glamorous horse with long, brunette hair, the red shoes with four-inch heels attached to wooden legs by ankle straps, and a pair of sunshades to protect her delicate eyes. Carol made sure Priscilla was at dinner just late enough to be seen by all. Some would say Priscilla was *fashionably late.*

The waiters really got into the spirit of Priscilla. I heard one waiter whisper, *"By golly, if a horse can wear a wig and sun shades, I can too!* He transcended an initial shyness, and approached our tables. *"Could I try on Priscilla's wig?"* Permission was granted, despite the fact that Priscilla seemed a bit annoyed. Some even swear they heard a faint, *"Neigh"*, translated *"NO!"* in English. The waiter took the wig anyway and smiled broadly as he served our food, long dark hair flowing. We never knew whether the waiter was among the 4% of men who have an interest in exploring the feminine, thought the idea was a funny joke, or actually wanted to participate in the camaraderie he had observed at our tables.

By then the positive mood had begun to spread. Several other waiters came to our tables and asked, *"How many wigs can you round up for the waiters?"* As you might expect, there were several available, so the next night the passengers experienced the parade of Baked Alaska carried by waiters with beautiful hair. All managed to keep the hair away from the flames! The dining room lights were turned down low, but the passengers began to notice the waiters who had accepted our group!

WHEN MACHO MEETS FEMININE

Meanwhile at the other end of the dining room there were two other groups: the staff from a dental office and a golf team. The two groups began to affectionately call us, "*The group having all the fun.*" They also noticed that we were the group bonded by a rare form of unconditional love!

The next day the golf team was searching frantically for us. They had an urgent request and time was running out! It seems one of the wives in the dental group had a birthday the next day. Her husband mused, "*What if I dress as a woman and surprise her? What better gift could I give her? She will see that I am not afraid visit Venus!*" He didn't expect what happened next! When he was halfway in his transformation from Martian to Venusian, a second member of the group asked to have a transformation also.

The mood was set, and the plans were made. Just a few minutes after dinner began the two men entered the room, each dressed to the nines, both wearing broad smiles, and one carrying a birthday cake with an undisclosed number of flaming candles. Our group was already in place in a circle around the table, ready to sing, *Happy Birthday*. The crowd joined in with laughter when the husband of the birthday girl pushed his right sleeve up to show a tattoo which had been painted onto his muscular upper arm. His message came through loud and clear. "*Hey! You guys out there. I am all man, but it is OK for a Martian to visit Venus. The softer side feels nice.*"

Something magical began to happen! A wave of support spread through the dinning room. Passengers stood to their feet to give an ovation. When the staff turned on the music, dancing broke out all across the huge room. We felt the inhibitions drop like a giant thud clearly heard through the formal atmosphere. The music in the air was not chamber music one would expect in an environment in which the mood is set by candlelight and roses. We found ourselves rocking to the sounds which screamed out, "*Move away from stereotypes. Join in the fun! Life is too short for inhibitions. Life is fun on another planet!*"

SUPPORT GROWS FROM DIGNITY

By then our group was firmly bonded to the dental office and the macho guys from the golf team. We even joined in when they bellowed, "*Macho, Macho, Macho Man!*" About this time a plan started to form. All three groups would come to dinner, in mass, dressed in toga. The next night, about an hour before dinner, we gathered in one of the cabins to get dressed in the flowing gowns made of white bed sheets borrowed from the cabin boys. Observers watched our wives as they demonstrated love and support for their husbands. Each of us made sure the robes were beautifully draped, all hair was in place under the head piece, and no straps were showing on the bare shoulders.

Then, at the appointed time, all three groups entered. There were no distinct lines separating the transgendered from golfers and the dental staff. The groups had bonded, and we moved as one. Once again, the other people on board were moved as well, and the *ice* was broken. Laughter replaced the more subdued mood of formal dining, and support continued to grow.

The following morning the Purser's office told us they had been swamped with requests from passengers in the first sitting to be changed to late sitting. Word was out that the *neatest folks on board were in our group.*

Our experience reached a climax on the night of the talent show. Jody had entered a few days before. What we did not know, however, was that the entertainers on board had given Jody an extra measure of coaching. Other contestants preceded her, and sang in average voices center stage, with little animation. Then it happened! Jody was announced by the Cruise Director, the curtain lifted, and Jody appeared like a beauty queen. Standing within a beautiful back drop of stars, she gracefully moved before us. The stage crew released the smoky fog from beneath the floor as she began a sultry lip synch to full orchestration. She moved through the audience, gently stroking the bald heads she found in her path, and perched upon a lap or two. The crowd roared! When the song had ended, everyone was standing in a dramatic gesture of approval.

At the conclusion of the act Jody led everyone in *Happy Birthday* as one of the female entertainers approached the front of the auditorium. Our group gathered around as a tee shirt was presented to honor her special day. The inscription read, "*I was born a Venusian, but I really want to be a Martian!*" Then the truth came out. When the entertainer joined the crew, she had very short hair, and the other entertainers gave her a masculine name. "*So!*" Jody explained. "*We have just made you an honorary member of the gender community as a female to male crossdresser, and a citizen of Planet Mars*!" The entertainer blushed, the crowd roared, and everyone in our group felt a rare satisfaction and joy!

A still silence fell over the crowd as Jody took her place center stage. Her voice dropped into a mellow baritone as she spoke. "*As you already know, I am Jody but I am also John. I am a man who was born with a very large feminine side, and I express the feminine side with clothing. Our group would like to say,'Thank you,' to all 1400 of you who have opened your hearts to us. You have accepted us and you have shown us that you are capable of moving beyond the social mores which sometimes control our lives. We love you for this. The group joins me in gratitude, for it is sometimes difficult living on two planets!*"

If there had been any dry eyes in the crowd, they were dry no more. Slowly, the crowd rose to their feet, wiped the tears from their eyes, and started to move toward us. The comments warmed our hearts. Some said, *"You taught us much about life."* Others said, *"This cruise was boring until we found you."* A few women said, *"When we get home, we are going shopping for large-size dresses then we'll know **Who's Really from Venus!** "*

The next day it was time to pack for home. Priscilla, Queen of the Seas, was returned to the prop room, but her red high heels and wig went back home with Jody and Char. Oh! by the way. Priscilla was not a winner in the races held at pool side. She only showed in the second race. But, let me tell you, our gender community was the winner! In the future, many people will view us differently. This all happened because a group of women chose to share the experience with their husbands. It is true! The open hand holds more love than the closed fist.

FOR INFORMATION ABOUT DIGNITY CRUISES :

Contact: PM Publishers,
P.O. Box 5304
Katy, Texas 77491-5304
Fax your request for information to: 281-347-8747
Or visit our web site: http://www.pmpub.com

Is this the original SPICE Girl?

CHAPTER ELEVEN
THE ORIGINAL SPICE GIRLS

*T*he most difficult part of dealing with the phenomenon of crossdressing relates to the process of sorting fact from fiction, and feelings from fears. But successful coping strategies are possible if enough information is available and if people take advantage of resources. SPICE, or Spouses' and Partners' International Conference for Education, contributes significantly, since the program format is designed to:

1. *Enhance communication between couples,*
2. *Promote respect within relationships individuals,*
3. *Encourage the renewal of lifelong friendships, and*
4. *Increase an awareness of human need and responsibility.*

While the conference is wonderful for mending broken hearts, SPICE has an equally important purpose directed toward the loving couples who want to grow closer. Programs presented at SPICE are based upon the perceived needs of participants. Men and women have separate, yet parallel, programs with some programs designated for application and closure for couples and women who attend alone. Personal and relationship development is the goal.

A PARTICIPANT REMEMBERS SPICE

During SPICE in Ontario, California, in July, 1997, I frequently observed Dana in the hotel lobby writing in his journal. Dana, a tall, handsome man with dark curly hair, and an open, friendly face seemed more serious and less animated on Saturday than he had earlier in the week. I stopped to greet him. *"Good afternoon, Dana. You look very busy!"*

Dana described his desire to capture thoughts and emotions while they were still fresh. *"We've been through therapy of various kinds and I had a bout with severe depression. We realized moving away from crossdressing was not going to be an option if we wanted to have a chance at a full, happy life. I really don't want to lose a single thought, because I have found many answers during the conference!"* Dana's introspection was reflected in his journal. The manuscript, which was later widely distributed on the internet, described his thoughts about SPICE, himself, his endless journey between Venus and Mars and his love relationship.

DETAILS AND OVERALL THOUGHTS ABOUT SPICE

I'm a heterosexual crossdresser. I've been married to my wife, Kiki, for twelve years, and it took six years before I told her about my crossdressing. We negotiated an agreement. I travel to Reno, the nearest city, every couple of months to a safe transformation shop. I have an evening with other crossdressers and spend the night. I never go anywhere alone, but Kiki has never seen my femme side, the pictures en femme, or any of my femme clothing.

In April of 1997, I attended the International Foundation for Gender Education (IFGE) Convention on the Queen Mary in Long Beach. That experience, along with the closeness I've developed with my new friends in Reno and on the internet, made me believe my feminine side was becoming more a part of our lives. We talked about going to SPICE, and Kiki agreed we should try it. We flew down to Ontario, California, with quite a bit of apprehension, and little or no preconceptions. Among other things, this would be the first time Kiki would ever knowingly meet another crossdresser.

In summary, SPICE was wonderful. That doesn't mean it was the perfect conference; there is no such thing, and it would certainly be impossible with such an incredibly diverse group of people. I had read negative stories about SPICE - husbands being verbally bashed, or the participants being accosted with only one way of doing things. I want to tell you up front that none of that happened. There was love and mutual support all around. Not that there wasn't tension. There were some couples having some pretty deep crises, and the knowledge that the wives were talking about us in the next room as we were discussing them, automatically raised feelings in me. I found myself thinking, "*What are they laughing about in there?*" This, I was told, was a good sign, for in other years the women were not yet in the mood to laugh and be happy. But in this conference every person there was sufficiently committed to their relationship to be spending time, money, and tremendous emotional energy to improve their ability to love and be loved! My life was enriched by meeting other couples who shared the kind of love Kiki and I had always enjoyed. Observing those who had successfully negotiated the issues was encouraging!

GETTING TO KNOW YOU

Kiki and I didn't know what to expect from SPICE, or from ourselves. We had a vague notion that we were doing this to improve our twelve-year marriage, but we had no idea how SPICE might help us do that. Even now, after the conference, whether it has any lasting impact is entirely up to us. We know the presenters did their part beautifully. But time will tell if our own personal experience is a major turning point or just a bump in the road. But, at least, we've pulled out the road map.

On Thursday the conference theme, **GETTING TO KNOW YOU**, was taking on new meaning. Somewhat to our surprise, the wives and husbands had their own program tracks for much of the time. Let me note here that some women, attending alone, were in their own set of workshops. I rarely saw some of them; don't even know how many there were. Our first workshop involved breaking into pairs. We introduced ourselves to one new friend and talked a few minutes; then the group came back together and we introduced our friend to the group. Some of us were there for the first time, but many of the participants had been to every SPICE. Tremendous diversity among the men was quickly obvious. There were cross-dressers (CD's) whose wives had never seen them dressed, others whose wives help them dress, CD's who went out more than once a week, and some who hadn't dressed in months. There was one transsexual and one in transition.

If I had any questions about whether this group of strangers would be willing to share their innermost thoughts and feelings, they were eliminated right then and there. Although the stereotypical man from Mars does not speak openly or easily about personal issues, that sure didn't hold for this group! After all, we've all had lots of practice working with our feminine selves. You'd think a group of people, acquainted for less than a week, might have trouble opening up, but this was not true at SPICE. We were beginning to see the advantages to traveling the endless journey between Venus and Mars. We were learning that all of us have both masculine and feminine energies within, and our relationships are better when we draw from the *gender bank.*

SEX AND INTIMACY

I remember starting to scratch the surface of our marital relationship in the workshop, *Sex and Intimacy,* but not getting into it very far. When looking back to the conference holistically, it seems the programs were structured somewhat like bricks, with each one building on the previous one. The most important point of this session was in the title itself, *Sex and Intimacy.* The two words represent two tightly related subjects, but they're not the same thing.

Many couples who think they're having sexual difficulties are really having difficulties being intimate with each other! Of course, couples that are not transgendered (TG) also have trouble really being intimate.

But TG couples have another problem to overcome. There's this third person, the TG's feminine self, hanging around the fringes. A lot of the discussion, in this workshop and others having to do with sex, centered on the issue of the crossdressing in bed, and/or dressing for lovemaking. It almost seemed to be a foregone conclusion that every crossdresser wants to make love with his wife while crossdressed. I felt a bit out of it, because that particular desire is not on my wish list, but it was one of the earliest indications to me of how different we all are. It seems obvious that the couples who experience sex as a part of the crossdressing experience have pushed the boundaries back further than Kiki and I have, and there seemed to be a problem for some of the women as they tried to integrate sex and the gender issue.

GETTING TO KNOW YOURSELF

The first session with Walter Bockting, from the University of Minnesota Medical School, really began to go deeply into relationship issues and how our transgendered (TG) status impacts them. So many of our difficulties arise from problems in communication, which is made more difficult, in turn, by the different ways men and women communicate!

Martians, for example, get virtually all their information in a conversation from the words said. Venusians get far more of their information from perception, the visual cues of the other person. Walter gave us the following model for discussing relationship issues with our partners, and a couple of the men tried a demonstration for us. I'm presenting it as initiating with the man, but it could start either way.

Step One: Describe The Situation

Tell your partner what you see as the status quo. *"Dear, our kids don't know about me. They're getting older now, and I think it might be time to tell them."*

Step Two: Describe Your Feelings About This

"I feel separated from them, since they don't know all about their dad. And I have a real fear that they may stumble on to it some other way. That could really be damaging to the trust they have in me, and in us."

Step Three: Tell What You Need From Her

Be very specific about this - try to present a need that will be possible. *"I'd like you to start thinking about telling the kids sometime, even if it's some years from now. Maybe we can pick a time next week for you and me to talk about this some more."*

The partner comes back with a paraphrase of what you said; her understanding of it, anyway. That's important. If she didn't understand it correctly, you can get into a discussion about the wrong thing!

Persons using the technique must try to avoid the confrontational aspects of negotiating. That is a trap in many relationships, whether or not crossdressing is involved. We're working together on marriage, after all.

There was some discussion about how we physically place ourselves for discussions. I, for example, don't do well sitting directly across from Kiki, since it feels too much like we're in emotional opposition to each other. In our session on Saturday, we pulled our chairs almost right next to each other, our hips almost touching.

Walter gave us some homework. We were to come to the session on Friday with some issues to discuss using the model. As the conference continued there was an occasional use of role-playing, mixed with explanations by the presenters and personal stories from the participants. The men got to know each other quite well. We also understood the nature of each relationship.

When Kiki and I compared notes at the end of each day, it became apparent that, in some cases, the man's description of what was going on in the relationship did not jibe very well with that of his wife! The need for better communication between married partners was brought home to us in a very real way.

Kiki and I missed the evening programs on Thursday and Friday, and there were numerous other programs not discussed here including, *Getting to Know Your Partner,* Growing Together *and Not Apart, Will it Ever Be Easy?* There were also several panel discussions. We were especially sorry to miss Richard Miller's presentation Friday evening but we did buy Rachel Miller's book, **THE BLISS OF BECOMING ONE**. The other couples thought the evening program was great.

I felt pretty intense on Saturday. This was the morning for a final check of what we'd learned about communicating with our partners, in preparation for actually putting it into practice that afternoon. Following lunch, all the couples convened. After a short introduction, we paired off with our wives and significant others

(SO's). I presented my issue to Kiki, using the model we'd learned. She listened, and paraphrased it back to me. I corrected a couple of details, and we talked about how to accomplish what I asked in a *win-win* kind of way. My issue related to how hard it is for me to bring up TG issues with her. It always raises a big red flag. I fear she may think I'm about to ask her if I can do something new; push the barriers back a bit further. I asked if we could set a weekly time that would always be open to discuss these issues, or anything else really personal about our relationship. I'm happy to say we are now doing that.

Kiki took her turn, and that went well, too, but I'll keep what she asked confidential. The same process was going on all over the room. Although I didn't hear any of these conversations, the couples were obviously taking the exercise seriously and really trying to accomplish something. I felt very proud of all of us! Finally, after a break, we were all together once again.

Kiki and I ran to the airport after this session. There was no real presentation during the last meeting time, but rather questions and comments from various people around the room. The idea was to bring together everything that had happened in the past three days. Is that all it was? Our staff made sure we had some real tools we could take home with us.

The name of the game for Kiki and me, as well as some others, was relationship building. There's this Venusian part of my personality, that can create a distance. Potentially, it can keep us from being as close and intimate with each other as we'd both like. So, the idea is to find ways that Kiki can allow the Venusian side into the relationship in a way that is within her comfort zone. Improving our relationship is about caring and sensitivity to the needs of each other. It is also about being respectful of feelings.

By Dana Bourne

THE BIRTH OF A LEADER

I met Desir`ee Leigh the first day of our 1996 SPICE in Wilmington, Delaware. Her smile was like an oasis! She found me rushing about trying to finish all the last minute details involved in a conference of this magnitude. I remember her warm personality, and willingness to help! We were instant friends. Within a week after the close of the conference Desiree' had written her thoughts about the conference. Here is her story:

I have only been aware of the gender gifted community for about three years. When I learned that SPICE (Spouses and Partners International Conference on Education) was going to have their meeting in July this year. I wanted to go so that I could learn more about the gender gifted.

I arrived early so that I would have plenty of time to meet others as they arrived. Unfortunately, I became ill during the cruise and spent most of my energy trying to *make it through the night.* At about 3 AM I couldn't stand it any longer and went to the hospital. The doctors couldn't determine exactly what was the matter so they sent me back to the hotel with a handful of reports to take to my own doctor at home. Unfortunately this little excursion caused me to miss the opening of the convention.

The morning sessions, which I missed, contained discussions on the following issues: *Nature of Crossdressing; Concerns About the Children; Boundaries and Conflict Resolution; Relationship Building; Gender Differences and Communication; Sex, Gender, and Bedroom Issues.*

I was able to participate in the afternoon sessions and the next three days of meetings. Some of the sessions included: *Ask Your Doctor, Minister, Psychotherapist, and Friend; Secrets, Honesty and Risks; Speaking from the Heart; What You Always Wanted To Know but Were Afraid to Ask; and Where Do We Go From Here?* These sessions were led by professionals and assisted by members of the transgender community.

I was impressed with the women who attended; their openness, and their friendliness. There were meetings for women only, for men only and for men and women together. The luncheons were segregated by sex also, so that the participants would feel free to converse informally about the morning's subjects. Dinners were for everyone. The heart of all of this was the communication between the women at the conference. All of us have a story to tell and all of the stories are different. Yet the stories are of the same subject: living, loving and working in a relationship that transcends Venus and Mars. We talked with each other and found we were all searching for answers and understanding. The friendships which evolved will last a very long time, because we walk on a common ground. One of the special features was the opportunity to meet and discuss anything with anyone in the hospitality room. There were social activities, and each evening after dinner there was a speaker and entertainment.

I heartily recommend SPICE to any wife or significant other of a gender gifted male. They will be able to learn about both themselves and their mates and their relationship.

By Desir`ee

When I remember meeting Desir`ee and other wonderful women like her, an old saying comes to mind. *"The gold of friendship is a golden thing. The more we spend it on each other, the richer we become."*

RACHEL REMEMBERS SPICE

Rachel remembers many new experiences during SPICE, including her participation in bio- energetic exercise led by Melody Golden, a therapist in the Los Angeles area. Bio energetic exercise explains personality in terms of the body and its energetic processes. The activity is a form of therapy that combines work with the body and the mind. Many people who master the technique are able to resolve their emotional problems and realize more of their potential for pleasure and joy in living. A fundamental thesis of bio-energetic exercise is that the body and mind are functionally identical; that is, what goes on in the mind reflects what is happening in the body and vice versa. Unfortunately for Rachel, there are no counselors available in her area that are skilled in bio-energetic exercise, but other life changes occurred which will enhance her life. In the following account Rachel describes how SPICE changed her life:

I went to SPICE with the burden that the survival of my marriage was depending on me! In one of our many discussions about crossdressing, my husband had said, *"Things have to change or we go our separate ways."* Well, I figured I had to change. SPICE showed me that the burden of the marriage is shared between us! It's not all up to me!

This statement seems so simple, but it was like a revelation to me. A great burden was lifted! The actual meeting of other significant others was uplifting. I found it educational to realize other *normal* women were having difficulties coping with a Martian who prefers life on Venus. I had often thought there must be something wrong with me because I can't accept this. So just meeting these women helped immensely. I met one woman that seemed to have everything together, but she had previously been described as *a basket case* so I reasoned that there must be hope for me.

I felt sorry for the people that sat at my table that first night because I was crying already. It was just such a relief to be able to talk with someone about this. The online forum is great and has certain advantages if a person wants to be hidden, but meeting someone in person has a distinct advantage.

We learned about assertiveness, about setting boundaries, negotiating, and active listening. These are things that help you in everyday life. Such skill goes beyond coping with the Mars Venus analogy.

A big thing for me was going by myself. Initially, 1 wanted my husband to attend but that didn't work out so I went by myself. And it became my big adventure!! I proved to myself that I could do something I wasn't used to doing. I went outside my comfort zone. I realized that if worse comes to worse I can go my separate way and survive. I'll be okay. Once I realized this, it was only a short jump and I realized that if I stay in the relationship it will be because I want to stay, not because I am afraid of leaving! The taking of hormones was the big topic, and this proved to me that some women had more concerns than I did.

One group meeting was with a panel comprised of three crossdressers. They answered questions from the group of wives. I asked a question. This was totally out of character for me. *"When do I get to see this softer, more side of my husband? When he writes about crossdressing, it usually brings out his macho side and rarely his feminine side."*

The panel said it sounded like he had some work to do about integrating his masculine and feminine sides. A little light came on! I had work to do to improve me and our relationship, but he had work to do, too! He wasn't Mr. Perfect or even Miss Perfect.

Some of these things are so simple, so elementary, that you would think that they would be obvious. But they weren't obvious to me. I'm going to do my best to be at every SPICE! Perhaps there are more things to discover!

by Rachel

CONFERENCE AFTERGLOW

Since SPICE there have been many life changes. Dana says, "*A tangible change since SPICE is that I feel more open to talk with Kiki about TG issues, both light and heavy. She has even brought subjects up a few times since we've been back, which virtually never happened before. That makes me feel wonderful! SPICE was worth the time, money and emotional energy for us.*" Rachel is enjoying the awareness that she is not totally responsible for the success or failure of her marriage. I have appointed Desir`ee to the SPICE Planning Board, and she is skillfully using the leadership skill I saw that first day we met.

FOCUS AND PURPOSE

1. **SPICE**, or **SPOUSES' AND PARTNERS' INTERNATIONAL CONFERENCE FOR EDUCATION**, grew from the need for human interaction among the wives and partners of crossdressers. SPICE provides a secure environment where people can share ideas, learn from each other, and develop friendships. Crossdressers and their family members are encouraged to attend. Each year children of crossdressers have been in attendance.

2. SPICE is a celebration of the uniqueness found within our community, as well as a source of answers to the difficult questions which grow from the uniqueness.

3. SPICE guides participants to draw strength from one another but presents inner-strength as the primary answer to the problems experienced in life.

4. An ongoing input from the SPICE Planning Board, as well as from conference participants, has been the guiding force when the speakers are selected and programs are planned and implemented.

5. Each year the program format includes a couple's focus as well as programs for women who attend SPICE without partners.

6. In addition to the professional staff there are certified therapists present and available for crisis intervention.

At the conclusion of SPICE many thoughtful participants wrote notes of appreciation. One note was especially meaningful for me, since it was written by a lovely couple who had never attended any gender event. Their nervousness and anxiety were obvious just under the surface of their smiles. Their letter read as follows:

Dear Peggy,

It is difficult to write this note, for I am struggling to hold back the tears. We returned home from SPICE with our hearts full of gladness and hope. While we have attended conferences all over the world, I feel this is clearly the most powerful. SPICE should be recommended by all medical agencies and all governments around the world. Perhaps the following poem by Patrick J. Hacker-Harber summarizes our thoughts:

No one can choose your mountain,
or tell you when to climb.
It's yours alone to challenge,
At your own pace and time.

With eternal gratitude,
D and G

For additional information about relationships, subscribe to the **SWEETHEART CONNECTION**, % Onnalee Graham, editor, P.O. Box 8591, Minneapolis, MN 55408.

For additional information on SPICE, write to: SPICE, P.O. Box 5304, Katy, TX 77491-5304. Visit our web site at http://www.pmpub.com.

CHAPTER TWELVE
SOUTHERN
C�MFORT
REAL LIVES

"Very early in their lives, most transvestites feel very isolated. Without fail, every transvestite I've ever spoken with says at one time, they thought they were the only person in the world who crossdressed. Try to imagine the immense feelings of loneliness and desperation that must cause. No one to share their feelings with. No one to turn to for help, or information, or consolation.

It all comes down to fear of rejection and loss of love. Everyone needs to be loved by someone. Being loved means that we are worthy human beings. No love means worthlessness and that is equal to being bad. Bad people deserve to be ounished. If no one is punishing us, we feel guilty about that, too, which is a form of self-punishment. Yet we are driven by our feelings and most often reject love when it is offered because we feel unworthy. The key is to break the chain."

JoAnn Roberts

*O*ne of the best ways for crossdressers and their partners to break the chain is by stepping away from loneliness and toward events designed for friendship. Sherri Shapiro observed people breaking the chain and tells about her experiences:

I had never had anyone ask me if I was a *real girl*. It was the second evening of Southern Comfort, a convention for crossdressers, transgenderists, and transsexuals held annually in Atlanta, Georgia. I was slightly taken aback by the question, but then I laughed and told my inquirer that everything about me was quite real, including, unfortunately, my big butt!

You may wonder what a single, straight female was doing at the conference. I was there because someone I love is transgendered, and attendance represented one more step in the direction of understanding. Although I always accepted the concept of gender preference, I wanted to gain new insight and wisdom.

The gender community was a world in which I felt strangely comfortable. What seemed so complex to the masses had always been simple to me. I believe people have the right to achieve their human potential.

I came to the conference, on the first evening, to meet Tina, the femme side of the man I have been dating. We had planned to have a drink and visit with some of her friends - old and new alike. When I first walked into the Holiday Inn Conference Center Bar, I looked around to see if there were other genetic females present. By physical appearances, the answer seemed to be "*No.*" Over the next few days, however, I met some wonderful people and discovered there were more people than I had suspected who were, save for the packaging, like me. The very first person I met was to become a new friend. Her name was Ashleigh, and we bonded almost immediately. We have seen each other, spoken live and via e-mail several times since the conference.

Every person I met had a story. Despite the struggles of trying to fit into the world, or change it, most seemed happy and well-adjusted. Everyone seemed to have a family, although the families varied widely in knowledge and acceptance. Everyone struggled with the dissonance between outward appearance and inward reality - just like me. Everyone there was loving and needed love - just like me. And, as Tina had taught me, "*You don't always love a gender; you love a person.*" There was certainly a lot of love, support and camaraderie at the conference.

As at every conference I had ever attended, though the seminars, workshops, and speeches had value, the really important *stuff* was happening in the free time and social events. That was the real opportunity for people to come together and help each other heal, be resources for information, help a new person come out, share an experience with someone who had passed through a stage you were approaching, touch a life, and make a friend.

I came back on the second night for the dinner and talent show, as Tina was one of the lovely entertainers. It was a wonderful evening, with some very talented performers. But the talent or lack of it didn't matter. What really mattered was the courage everyone exhibited, the freedom of expression, the love and support ladled out by the encouraging audience, and the vicarious thrills received through the performances of others. People were looking around, admiringly and enviously. "*Maybe that will be me next year up there on that stage; maybe I will have journeyed to a new and better stop on my train of life, maybe I'll have made one new friend to support me, maybe I will stop one heart from breaking.*" So much poignancy, tears, and laughter!

As I looked around the room, the thing that made me sad was that I didn't see very many friends and spouses of all of these special people. I wondered how women could love someone and, despite personal pain, not try to be there for them. I believe real love is generous of spirit. Love is wanting everything for the one special person in your life's journey. Love is acceptance even in the absence of understanding. As Mary Chapin Carpenter said, *"There is a life we are given and one we choose."* The people present at Southern Comfort were given a unique gender preference. They could choose to express femininity or suppress it.

AUTHOR'S PERCEPTIONS

What was a woman like Sherri doing at this conference? First, I believe she was there to show support to one special person in her life, but she found herself reaching out to others who faced the struggle for self-acceptance and love. Her expressions of friendship brought her into a larger circle, an extended gender family.

Sherri was there to observe the expression of femininity, which did not seem to be dependent upon female genitalia. She found a rare bond with the Martians who prefer to live a part of life on Venus. As a participant she became a part of life's tapestry, a rare art form woven with the threads of contrast and diversity.

FOR A COMPLETE LIST OF GENDER EVENTS CONTACT:

International Foundation for Gender Education, (IFGE)
P.O. Box 229
Waltham, Massachusetts 02254-02229

Fax your request for information: 617-899-5703
or call 617-894-8340
E-mail: IFGE@ world.std.com
Web site: http://www.ifge.org

Barbara Jean has sketched a beautiful, young woman
as she prepares to attend Southern Comfort.

CHAPTER THIRTEEN
SUPPORT ORGANIZATIONS

"My own experience with self-acceptance was a journey accomplished very slowly over the past twenty nine years. Even now, though willing to tolerate society, I am unwilling to accept the wrath of my wife, and completely unwilling to subject my daughters to scorn or ridicule for having a crossdresser for a father. So perhaps until society is better educated in the issues, I may not have achieved self-acceptance, since I retain consideration for the small segment of the public, my nuclear family."

Thoughts by Diane from the book, **CROSSDRESSING WITH DIGNITY**

*T*he gender community has taken many giant steps since the day I received the emotional letter from Diane. Today there are a number of support organizations worldwide that can offer reassurance to women like Diane's wife and daughters. Crossdressers and their families are being guided toward inner harmony and peace. Organizations are reaching out into the world with the message: *human life is better when we draw our experiences from both Venus and Mars.*

The forward motion has propelled many leaders into the mainstream for the purpose of education and public awareness. Unlike the perceptions of Diane, we now know that individuals can do much to affect society. Three transgendered individuals, Brandi Welch, Dana Danahey, and Judy Daniels have carried the banner of dignity out into the world with educational programs designed for public schools as well as for colleges and universities. I became aware of the progress of these dedicated individuals when the University of Maine listed my book, **CROSSDRESSERS: AND THOSE WHO SHARE THEIR LIVES,** as a text for a class in human sexuality and gender issues. The more dramatic progress was evident when the producers of the Leeza Gibbons Show on NBC asked me to be a consultant for the program titled, *My Husband Wears My Clothes*, filmed at Paramount Studio in Hollywood. The program has been shown multiple times and has been seen by millions. The stigma has begun to dissolve!

Today many wives have found benefit in having a partner who co-exists on Venus and Mars. Some wives have assumed leadership roles.

The classic example is Frances Fairfax, who serves on the International Board of Directors of Tri-Ess and SPICE. She summarized the philosophy of Tri-Ess as follows:

"At Tri-Ess, we believe that crossdressing can be done with dignity, and without sacrificing any of the moral values you hold dear. Crossdressers are simply ordinary people with an extra facet that allows them to explore the feminine side of their personalities. If you explore and develop those feminine potentials, and balance and integrate them with your masculinity, you can find a happiness and fulfillment you hardly thought possible."

Frances obviously understands and accepts the Venusian heritage of her husband!

HELP FROM ORGANIZATIONS

Organizations and support services are growing in the fertile soil of acceptance under the direction of skilled leaders like JoAnn Roberts, founder of Creative Design Services and co-founder of Renaissance Education Association, and Melanie Rudd, founder of PM Publishers. JoAnn and Melanie describe their mission. *"We are committed to serving the needs of the gender community."* This statement summarizes the goals of all people who dedicate enormous amounts of time and talent in an effort to bridge the gap between dissonance and understanding.

The International Foundation for Gender Education (IFGE) is the largest non-profit organization serving the transgendered community. The goals of IFGE include:

- *To educate members of the transgender (TG) community, the general public, media, and elected officials on cross-dressing, transgender, and transsexual issues.*

- *To educate medical, psychological, and psychiatric health-care professionals about TG facts, needs, and special issues.*

- *To monitor legislation that affects the TG community.*

- *To provide outreach and referrals for organizations.*

The Society for the Second Self, Inc., Tri-Ess, is also an international, nonprofit, volunteer organization. The goal of Tri-Ess is to provide accurate informational and educational resources about the phenomenon of crossdressing and crossdressers. Tri-Ess seeks to promote understanding, acceptance, tolerance and a constructive public and self-image. Services by Tri-Ess reach out to crossdressers and their wives and partners. The informational and support activities also extend to the parents, children, other family members and friends of the crossdresser. The educational and informational resources are made available to educators, researchers, mental and physical health care professionals, employers, clergy, law enforcement and public officials, vendors, and the general public. The Tri-Ess philosophy, as articulated by Jane Ellen Fairfax, Chairperson of the Board, is the acronym FIBER, F- I- B- E- R:

"F - Full personality expression, in a blending of both our masculine and feminine characteristics. We do not wish to destroy our masculinity, but to soften its harsher aspects, and be all we can be.

I - Integration of our masculinity and femininity to create a happier, more complete, person as we use our enhanced under-standing of ourselves in our daily lives.

B - Balance between masculinity and femininity in our total personalities.

E - Education of crossdressers toward self-acceptance, education of our families toward understanding, education of society toward the acceptance of crossdressers as ordinary people with a special gender gift.

R - Relationship- building in the context of crossdressing."

Based upon these FIBER concepts, the organization uses all available resources to achieve its purpose. Programs and activities include charitable, educational and literary services such as the translation of literature into foreign languages. Other programs include the Pen Pal Program, and a membership directory. Tri-Ess assists local chapters and sponsors two international conferences each year, the Holiday En Femme, and the Spouses' and Partners' International Conference for Education (SPICE). More recently internet home pages have been established.

Tri-Ess, IFGE, Renaissance, and other organizations around the world, serve as an effective voice of advocacy for the trans-gendered. In recent years the groups have shared a community outreach booth at professional conventions, such as the American Psychiatric Association and the National Association of Social Workers. Groups have also supported the International Conference on Transgender Law and Employment Policy (ICTLEP) and the ITA and Gender PAC lobbying efforts. PM Publishers, under the direction of Melanie Rudd, has operated booths at several Conventions for the American Book Sellers Association.

Tri-Ess, IFGE and Renaissance are members of the World Congress of Transgender Organizations. There is a long history of cooperation, tolerance and understanding within a community of diversity. If you would like more information about Tri-Ess, Renaissance, or IFGE, or if you would like to join in supporting the work of these organizations, please write to:

The Society For The Second Self, Inc.
8880 Bellaire Blvd., B2, Suite 104,
Houston, Texas 77036-4621
Telephone: 713-349-8969
E-mail: TRIESSINFO@aol.com
Web site: http://www.triess.com

International Foundation for Gender Education
Box 229,
Waltham, Massachusetts 02254-0229
E-mail IFGE @WORLD.STD.COM
Web site: http://www.ifge.org

Renaissance
P.O. Box 61263,
King of Prussia, PA.19406

Spouses and Partners Support (SPICE)
P.O. Box 5304
Katy, Texas 77491-5304

EPILOG

by Jane Ellen Fairfax, M.D.

So who's really from Venus? Conventional wisdom connects women with Venus and men with Mars. Men and women may indeed seem to live in different worlds. As Dr. Rudd implies, however, the matter is not as simple as it appears.

As C. S. Lewis describes it in his Space Trilogy, Mars is a planet of becoming, a very masculine world. Its various populations strive to attain the highest pinnacle of logic, to create the most aesthetic art. It is a cold, formal world, hidebound in some ways, whose inhabitants live below the surface. While Mars is in some ways unpleasant, it is also a world of accomplishment, orderliness, and nobility of spirit. Lewis's Venus, on the other hand, is a world of being. Living on floating islands, borne along willy-nilly by natural forces, the heroine is content to the enjoy the beauties of the moment. She delights in her world and its creatures, confidently awaiting whatever adventure the next wave may bring. As knowledge comes to her, she integrates it into her being without striving or demanding. When at last she is reunited with the King, secure in his love, her happiness is complete.

The Martian world of masculinity can be stifling. Being a denizen of this dominant world may sound exciting. After all, isn't it thrilling to be #1?But it is a world bound by stereotypes, where inhabitants huddle in insecurity for fear of being labeled weak and unworthy of their Martian heritage. Whirled in a 90 m.p.h. rat race, many secretly long for a place away from the hubbub. A fortunate few Martians, however, were born in Extraterrestrial Gender Space between Mars and Venus. Within them burns a Venusian heritage. Since they do not look or act like stereotypical Martians, they are often ostracized by those who proclaim themselves pure breeds. Because they look more like Martians than Venusians, it is hard for the gentler Venusians to accept them as bona fide members of their own race. Truly such men, known as crossdressers, are People Without a Planet.

Are crossdressers condemned, then, to wander forever the dark void between Venus and Mars? By no means! Crossdressers need not deplore their Martian background, or try to fool people into thinking they are really Venusians. How rewarding it can to use those Venusian clothes as a lens by which to focus on and develop the traits that go with them! There is no reason why a crossdresser cannot be content to merely be, to isolate times when he can leave the striving behind and concentrate on the beauty before him. When he hears a newborn baby cry, he can rejoice in the miracle of Life. When he spies the fuschia buds on the azaleas, he can gladly anticipate the upcoming riot of color. He need not let his Martian heritage make him impervious to the joy of being alive. No fear of macho stereotypes need block his soul from communion with his fellow creatures. He can use his Venusian heritage to gain victory over isolation and selfishness. *"How many ears must one man have before he can hear people cry?"* Only two, if he is listening.

It is in relationships that Mars and Venus come together. Love is a Venusian territory, and it is not surprising that Venus is better known than Cupid. Here is where the crossdresser can shine. If he can overcome the Martian desire to dominate and control, and mix Martian strength with Venusian compassion and humility, he will be a wonderful husband and father.

So why does every crossdresser not come forward and proclaim his dual heritage? The answer is fear. The macho world feels threatened by men who do not need to be #1 in all things. It enlists some powerful allies. Hard-eyed preachers hurl Mosaic Law prohibitions at them; conventional types attack their manhood; Martian media make them a mockery; fraternal organizations reinforce stereotypes; and sadly, even some Venusians wave *"Keep Away"* signs. But organizations such as Tri-Ess have built Space Stations between Mars and Venus. On these stations crossdressers can learn to develop their Venusian traits while maintaining all that is best of their Martian heritage. No longer need they be alone, lost in space. They can maintain homes on both Mars and Venus, and live in them happily ever after.

BIBLIOGRAPHY

Allen, Charles (1978) You Are Never Alone. New York: Fleming H. Revell, Inc.

Allen, Mariette Pathy (1989) Transformations: Cross-dressers and Those Who Love Them. New York: E. P. Dutton, Inc.

Bourne, Dana (1997) Thoughts on SPICE: The 1997 Annual Spouses and Partners International Conference for Education. In:http:www.geocities.com/WestHollywood/5819/spicycomments.htm.

Brierly, Harry (1979) Transvestites: A Handbook With Case Studies for Psychologists, Psychiatrists, and Counselors. Oxford: Pergamon Press.

Brownsmiller, Susan (1984) Femininity. New York: Linden Press.

Buckner, H. Taylor. The Transvestite Career Path. In *Psychiatry* (1970) Vol. 33, pp. 381-89.

Bullough, Vern L. (1976) Sexual Variance in Society and History. Chicago: University of Chicago Press.

Bullough, Vern L. and Bullough, Bonnie (1993) Cross-dressers, Sex, and Gender. Philadelphia: University of Pennsylvania Press.

Bullough, Vern L. and Weinberg, Thomas. Alienation, Self-Image, and the Importance of Support Groups. In *The Journal of Psychology and Human Sexuality* (1988) Vol. 1 (2), p 83.

Bullough, Vern L. and Weinburg, Thomas. Women Married to Transvestites: Problems and Adjustments. In *Journal of Psychology and Human Sexuality* (1988) Vol. 1, pp. 83-104.

Busgalio, Leo (1994) Born for Love. New York: Random House.

Bushong, Carl (1995) The Multi-Dimensionality of Gender. Tampa: The Tampa Stress Center, Inc.

Davenport, Charles. A Follow-up Study of 10 Feminine Boys. In *Archives of Sexual Behavior* (1995) Vol. 15 : pp. 511-17.

Dawson, Jim (1996) Brain Power. Minneapolis: *Stat Tribute*.

Diamond, Milton (1990) Bisexuals: A Biological Perspective, a paper read at the Third International Berlin Conference of Sexology.

Docter, Richard F. (1988) Transvestites and Transsexuals: A Theory of Cross-Gender Behavior. New York: Plenum Press.

Dunham, Wendy (1997) Biological Factors Influencing Gender. http://www.scc.net/wendy/biologic.html.

Fairfax, Jane Ellen. Telling Your Children. In *The Femme Mirror*, Frances Fairfax, General Editor (Fall, 1997) Vol.22, Issue 4

Fairfax, Mary Frances and Fairfax, Jane Ellen. (1994) Children of Crossdressers-Sailing an Unchartered Sea. An Unpublished Monograph.

Fairfax, Mary Frances, General Editor. SPICE Report by Rachel. In *The Femme Mirror* (1997) Vol. 22, Issue 4, p.36.

Feinbloom, Deborah H. (1976) Transvestites and Transsexuals. Seymore Lawrence: Delacorte Press.

Fitzgerald, Jennifer (1997) How I Came To Where I Am. http://www.geocities.com/WestHollywood/9268/alittle.htm.

Freud, Sigmund. New Introductory Lectures on Psycho-analysis. In *The Standard Edition of the Complete Psychological Works of Sigmund Freud*, James Stachey, General Editor. London: The Hogart Press and Institute of Psychoanalysis (1933) Vol. 22, p 113.

Gagne, Patricia. et al. Coming Out and Crossing Over. In *Gender and Society* (Aug.,1997) Vol. 11, No 4, pp. 478-508.

Goffman, Erving (1963) Stigma: Notes on the Management of Spoiled Identity. Englewood Cliffs, New Jersey: Prentice Hall.

Graham, Onnalee, General Editor. This "Giggle," From Caryl on the CDSO List Serve. In *The Sweetheart Connection* (Fall, 1997)Vol. 5, Issue 4.

Gray, John (1992) Men are From Mars, Women are From Venus: A Practical Guide for Improving Communication and Getting What You Want in Your Relationship. New York: Harper Collins.

Harrison, Isabelle and Harrison, Louise. The Sister Act. An unpublished paper presented at the 1998 SPICE, Atlanta, Georgia.

Huber, Joan and Spitze, Glenna (1983) Sex Stratification. New York: Academic Press.

Kaye, Vanessa and Kaye, Linda (1996) Life With Vanessa. Oklahoma City, Oklahoma: Kaye.

Kohlberg, Lawrence (1966) A Cognitive Development Analysis of Children's Sex Role Concepts. In *Sex Differences in Behavior*. New York: Wiley.

Kohlman, Lawrence and Ulian, Z. (1974) Stages in the Development of Psychlogical Concepts and Attitudes In *Sex Differences and Behavior.* New York: Wiley.

Landau, Elaine (1991) Colin Powell: Four Star General, Library Ed. (First Books-Bibliographies). New York: Franklin Watts, Inc.

Landers, Ann. An Answer to One Who Has Seen it All In California (Oct. 4, 1997) In *Corpus Christi Caller-Times.* Sec. B, p 4.

Lebovitz, Phil. Feminine Behavior in Boys: Aspects of Its Outcome. In *American Journal of Psychiatry* (April 1972) Vol.128, pp. 1283-89.

Leigh, Desiree. SPICE Report. In *The Sweetheart Connection*, Onnalee Graham, Editor (1996)Vol. 5, issue 1, pp. 1, 7.

Mason-Schrock, Doug. Transsexual's Narrative of the True Self. In *Social Psychology* (1996) Vol.59, pp.176-92.

McKensie, E.C. (1980) 1400 Quips and Quotes. Grand Rapids: Baker Book House Company.

Miller, Niela (1996) Counseling in Genderland: A Guide for You and Your Client. Boston, Massachusetts: Different Paths Press.

Miller, Rachel (1996) The Bliss of Becoming One. Highland City, Florida: Rainbow Books, Inc.

Modi, J. A Note on the Customs of the Interchange of Dress Between Men and Women. In *India* (1925) Vol 5: pp 115-17.

Moir, Anne and Jessel, David (1989) Brain Sex: The Real Difference Between Men and Women. New York: Bantam Doubleday Group, Inc.

Money, John (1980) Love and Love Sickness. Baltimore: Johns Hopkins University Press.

Money, John and Ehrhardt, A.A. (1972) Men and Women, Boys and Girls. Baltimore: Johns Hopkins University Press.

Money, John and Tucker, P. (1975) Sexual Signatures. Boston: Little Brown and Company.

Namaste, K. The Politics of Queer Theory: A Sociological Approach to Sexuality. In *Sociological Theory* (1994)Vol.12: p. 22.

Paoletti, Jo B. and Kregloh, Carol L. (1989) The Children's Department. In *Men and Women Doing the Part.* Washington, D.C. : The Smithsonian Press.

Peo, Roger (1987) Wives of Cross-Dressers: Isolated and Misunderstood. Unpublished Monograph.

Prince, Virginia (1971) How to Be Woman Though Male. Los Angeles, California: Chevalier Publications.

Prince, Virginia (1997) The Cross-Dresser and His Wife. Capistrano, California: Sandy Thomas Publications.

Prince, Virginia (1976) Understanding Crossdressing. Capistrano, California: Sandy Thomas Publications.

Prince, Virginia and Bentler, P.M. A Survey of 504 Cases of Transvestism. In *Psychological Reports* (1972) Vol.31: pp 903-917.

Raymond, Janice (1994) The Transsexual Empire: The Making of a She-Male. New York: Teacher's College Press.

Roberts, JoAnn (1995) Coping With Crossdressing: Tools and Strategies For Partners in Committed Relationships. King of Prussia: Creative Design Services.

Rowe, Robert J. (1997) Bert and Lori: The Autobiography of a Crossdresser. New York: Prometheus Press.

Rubin, Theodore I. (1990) Real Love: What It Is and How to Find It. New York: Continuum.

Rudd, Peggy J. (1995) Crossdressers: And Those Who Share Their Lives. Katy, Texas: PM Publishers.

Rudd, Peggy J. (1992) Crossdressing With Dignity: The Case for Transcending Gender Lines. Katy, Texas: PM Publishers.

Rudd, Peggy J. (1989) My Husband Wears My Clothes. Katy, Texas: PM Publishers.

Salmans, Sandra. Objects and Gender: When An It Evolves Into a He Or a She (Nov. 16, 1989) In *New York Times*, Sec, B p.3.

Sanford, John A. (1980) The Invisible Partners. New York: Paulist Press.

Sheehy, Gail (1977) Passages: Predictable Crises of Adult Life. New York: E. P. Dutton.

Stern, Karl (1975) The Flight From Woman. New York: Farrar, Strause, and Grant.

Stoller, Robert. Transvestite's Women. In *American Journal of Psychiatry* (Sep., 1967) pp.333-38.

Stone, Gregory (1982) Appearances and the Self In Life as A Theater. Chicago: Aldine Press.

Talamani, John (1982) Boys Will Be Girls: The Hidden World of Heterosexual Male Transvestites. Washington, D.C.: University Press of America.

Tannen, Deborah (1990) You Just Don't Understand. New York: William Morrow and Company.

Tewksbury, Richard, and Gagne', Patricia. Transgenderists: Products of Non-normative Intersections of Sex, Gender, and Sociology. In *Journal of Men's Studies* (1996) Vol.5: pp. 105-29.

Thorne, Peggy R. (1993) Love Calendar: The Secrets of Love. Katy, Texas: PM Publishers.

West, Candace, and Fenstermaker, Sarah. Doing Difference. In *Gender and Society* (1987) Vol. 9: pp. 8-37.

Whitman, Frederick L. and Zent, Michael. Cross-Cultural Assessment of Early Cross-Gender Behavior and Familial Factors in Male Homosexuality. In *Archives of Sexual Behavior* (1984) Vol.13: pp. 427-39.

Winokur, Jon (1989) Curmudgeon's Garden of Love. Markham, Ontario: Penguin Books.

Wise, Thomas, Dupkin, Carol and Myer, John. Partners of Distressed Transvestites, In *American Journal of Psychiatry* (Sep.,1981) Vol. 138: pp 1221-24.

Woodhouse, Annie (1989) Fantastic Women. New Brunswick, New Jersey: Rutgers University Press.

INDEX

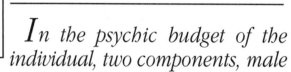

In the psychic budget of the individual, two components, male and female, must be linked in harmony.

Helen Deutsch

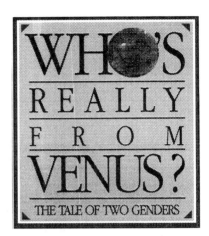

WH●'S
REALLY
FROM
VENUS?
THE TALE OF TWO GENDERS

"My books

are water;

those of the

great geniuses

are wine-

everybody

drinks water."

-Mark Twain

ORDER FORM -MAY BE DUPLICATED

_____ **MY HUSBAND WEARS MY CLOTHES.** $14.95

_____ **CROSSDRESSING WITH DIGNITY.** $12.95

_____ **LOVE CALENDAR.** Special price $6.95

_____ **CROSSDRESSERS: AND THOSE WHO SHARE THEIR LIVES.** $14.95

_____ **WHO'S REALLY FROM VENUS?** $15.95

_____ **TRANSFORMATIONS.** Special price $19.95

_____ Sub-total

_____ 10 % Discount for orders of 2 or more books

_____ Total after discount (if 2 or more books ordered)

_____ Sales Tax - Texas Residents add 08%

_____ Shipping 10% of total order domestic or 15% of total order for international. For air mail international add $3.00 each book.

_____ Total

You may pay by check, money order or credit card:

Credit card: (   ) Visa (   ) Mastercard (   ) Discover

(   ) American Express

Credit Card Number _____ Exp. _____

_____
Name (on Card)

_____
Street   City   State   Zip Code

Signature _____ Email _____

Send your check, MO or credit card order to: PM Publishers
P.O. Box 5304
Katy, TX 77491-5304
Fax (281) 347-8747

On-Line Secure orders: PM Publishers Web Site:
http://www.pmpub.com /books.htm